FREE AND INDEPENDENT

Other Books by Noel B. Gerson

FREE AND INDEPENDENT

The Confederation of the United States
1781–1789

by

Noel B. Gerson

THOMAS NELSON INC.

Camden   New York

First edition

Copyright © 1970 by Noel B. Gerson

Library of Congress Catalog Card Number: 77–119359

MANUFACTURED IN THE UNITED STATES OF AMERICA FOR
THOMAS NELSON INC.

*For
Anne
Wendy
Brennan*

CONTENTS

FREE AND INDEPENDENT

LAKE SUPERIOR

CANADA

(VERMONT)
Claimed by N. Y.,
N. H. & Mass.

(MAINE)

St. Croix R.

NORTHWEST
TERRITORY
Claimed by
Virginia
Ceded 1784

LAKE HURON

LAKE MICHIGAN

LAKE ONTARIO

NEW
YORK

N.H.

MASSACHUSETTS

RHODE
ISLAND

Claimed by Massachussetts and
Virginia   Ceded 1784 - 85

Claimed
by
N.Y. & Mass.

Claimed by Conn. & Virginia
Ceded 1784 - 86

LAKE ERIE

WESTERN
RESERVE
Ceded 1800

CONNECTICUT

PENNSYLVANIA

N.J.

Claimed by Virginia
Ceded 1784

MD.

DEL.

LOUISIANA

Mississippi R.

VIRGINIA

(KENTUCKY)
Claimed by Virginia
Admitted as state 1792

Claimed by North Carolina
Ceded 1790

NORTH CAROLINA

Ceded 1787

SOUTH
CAROLINA

ATLANTIC

OCEAN

Claimed by Georgia
Ceded 1802

GEORGIA

Claimed by Spain,
United States & Georgia

FLORIDA (Spanish)

St. Mary's R.

FLORIDA
(Spanish)

Apalachicola River

GULF
OF
MEXICO

BAHAMA
ISLANDS

CUBA

THE
UNITED STATES
DURING THE
CONFEDERATION
PERIOD

I. The Articles of Confederation—1781

We, the people of the United States, in order to form a more perfect Union, establish justice, insure domestic tranquility, provide for the common defence, promote the general welfare, and secure the blessings of liberty to ourselves and our posterity, do ordain and establish this Constitution for the United States of America.

These words, their purpose noble and their vision sweeping, make up the preamble of the Constitution of the United States. That great document created a new form of government that has endured from the time it was adopted in 1789 down to the present day. It is the heart, and perhaps the soul as well, of a nation dedicated to liberty, justice, and equality.

The Constitution did not come into being overnight, of course. It was the direct product of the two periods immediately preceding it. The first was the Revolution, formally known as the War of Independence, which broke out in 1775, when thirteen of Great Britain's seaboard

North American colonies rebelled. The second, which began while the war was still being fought, was the period of the Confederation of the United States.

The Confederation, itself a form of government, came into being in the spring of 1781, and remained in existence for eight years. Certainly it is not accidental that the Constitution's preamble called for "a more perfect Union." The trials the infant nation endured and the errors she made during the period of the Confederation—less than a decade—were so numerous that they could scarcely be counted. But the new nation discovered her strengths, too. More important, she learned how to use them. In the broadest sense, the era of the Confederation was a time of schooling for the people and their elected leaders. Victory was certain in 1781, and the existence of the country was formally recognized in the peace signed with Great Britain in 1783. But that was only the beginning.

It is not an exaggeration to say that the United States obtained her higher education during the years of the Confederation. England, as well as most of Continental Europe, was convinced that the United States would collapse. Her survival was said to be a miracle, a miracle brought about by the people of the United States. It began with the beginning of the war, but was performed principally during the time of the Confederation.

On July 4, 1776, when the elected representatives of the North American rebels declared their nation's independence, approximately 2,250,000 people lived in the thirteen colonies. Boston, the second-largest city, had fewer than sixteen thousand inhabitants. The largest city, Philadelphia, had a population of about twenty-five thousand, and New York, which was doomed to be occupied by the British for the better part of the war, had less than twenty thousand.

Most of the people were farmers who grew food for their own families. When there was a small surplus, it was sold in the cities and towns. There were virtually no factories of any consequence in the colonies; the Industrial Revolution was already making great strides across the Atlantic, but its influence had not yet been felt in the New World. Cloth was woven for home consumption. All ironware, including pots and pans, was imported. In fact, the only iron foundry in the new nation was located at Worcester, Massachusetts, so it was difficult at the beginning of the war for the rebels to forge their own cannon and ammunition.

Benjamin Franklin of Philadelphia had long owned the only printing presses on the American seaboard that could produce books. The paper used by the news organs of the larger cities was imported. Even medicines, other than local herbs, came from England and Europe.

The chief exports were "natural" products, timber from the limitless forests, and furs. But a lively foreign trade was growing. Shipowners in New England ports, among them Boston and Newport, Rhode Island, New Haven, and New London, sent their vessels to the West Indies and Europe. So did the proprietors of fleets in Philadelphia, New York, and Charleston, South Carolina. Many were prosperous, and merchant John Hancock of Boston was said to be the wealthiest man in the colonies.

"Our main products," wrote pamphleteer and editor Sam Adams on the eve of the Revolution, "are our love of liberty and our unquenchable hope for the future of this, our land."

By the end of 1780, the weary American people had learned that it was difficult to live on little but hope. The thirteen colonies had become states, and each was so jealous of its powers that virtually no real authority had been granted to the common government the colonies had been forced to form for the purpose of prosecuting the war. The Continental Congress, as the "national" government was called, was helpless.

Composed of delegates from each state, it was feeble in power. It printed paper money that was worth little more than the cost of the ink and the paper itself. Every state had reserved the right to print its own money, and to make coins as well, and so the Congress was given no gold or silver to back up its own money.

In other realms, the Congress was equally impotent. It could not pass or enforce legislation that would require the states to work together, either for the prosecution of the war or the planning of the peace. Although it appointed and supervised the activities of ambassadors, its rights to speak for all thirteen of the states in dealing with other powers was strictly limited.

Only in the field of military operations had necessity forced the states to grant the Congress a minimum of rights. The Continental Army reported to the Congress, which appointed and promoted its officers. But few funds were provided to pay that army's wages. And the militia of the states competed directly with the Continentals in recruiting men! It is small wonder that the "national" army, commanded by Major General George Washington, never numbered more than eleven thousand men.

It is equally remarkable that even that many men were willing to enlist in the Continentals and serve for the duration of the war. Not only were they paid in worthless Continental dollars while their families risked total neglect, but they endured hardships without end. Often no cloth was available for uniforms, no leather for boots, and food supplies were so meager that some troops literally starved.

Nevertheless the tide turned slowly in the favor of the American rebels. The victory achieved in 1777 by a corps of Continentals at the Battle of Saratoga in New York was the beginning. A few months later, Benjamin Franklin, the American envoy to France, persuaded the government of King Louis XVI to recognize the United States. France did far more than open formal diplomatic negotiations. She sent experienced troops and a powerful fleet to help the struggling Americans. Weapons, ammunition, cloth for uniforms, and all kinds of supplies began to come across the Atlantic in a steady stream.

Even more important, France became an active ally of the Americans when she declared war on Great Britain in 1778. Operations in Europe, close to home, were infinitely more important to her than the campaign in the distant New World. So pressure against the beleaguered rebels lessened as Army and Royal Navy troops were diverted elsewhere.

The United States continued to flounder, however, and by 1780 many of her people were in despair. Something had to be done on the political front as well as the military, the Continental Congress having become little more than a debating society. Prominent citizens throughout the country worked for the formation of a new, permanent government that would administer the nation's affairs. That government was the Confederation of the United States.

The Articles of Confederation, the "constitution" adopted by the thirteen states in March, 1781, provided a form of government that maintained the principles of the Continental Congress. In essence, thirteen independent nations banded together in an alliance, or confederation. The states remained unwilling to give up their sovereign powers to a government that would act on behalf of all the people in every state. The need to win the war, to establish a secure nation, and to protect the liberty for which so much had been sacrificed compelled the grudging states, however, to yield at least a few of their rights.

Each state elected representatives to a Continental Congress. That Congress, in turn, elected those who would serve the entire nation. For the first time a Ministry of Foreign Affairs was authorized, as was a Ministry of the Treasury, which would issue money and collect customs taxes authorized by the new Congress. A national judiciary was also created, for the purpose of settling legal disputes between the states. Unfortunately, these courts had no powers to enforce their decisions. But they did work, on a noncompulsory basis, to urge the states to adopt uniform criminal and other legal codes.

The Confederation took one very long step toward the creation of a truly national government. The new Congress was authorized to draw up laws for the entire United States. But bills passed by the Congress did not automatically become the law of the land. *The heart of the Articles of Confederation provided that no legislation, including the direction of the Ministries, would become law until ratified by nine of the thirteen states.*

The process of ratification was slow and cumbersome. And the approval of nine states was difficult to achieve, due to individual and regional differences. Those who favored a bill, on the one hand, and those who opposed it, on the other, gave in to the temptation to make "horse-trade" deals. Such deals were common whenever the Congress was meeting in Philadelphia, the national capital at the time. The representatives of Connecticut, for example, might say to those from Virginia, "Support our new bill, and we'll vote for your new bill."

The most glaring weakness in the Articles of Confederation was the refusal of the states to concede authority of any sort for the benefit of all states. The voice of any one state in the Continental Congress was as strong as that of any other state: each voted as a unit, abiding by the will of its *own* majority, and each had one vote in the Congress. Therefore, the newest state, Georgia, which was largely an uninhabited wilderness, had a vote equal to that of New York, Massachusetts, or Pennsylvania, where an overwhelming majority of the people lived.

Other weaknesses were less apparent but just as harmful. The Articles of Confederation made no provision for the establishment of a real executive branch of the government. This failure deprived the nation of the vigorous leadership it so badly needed.

An obvious example demonstrates the point. Virginia, where the first permanent settlement was made in 1607, had developed a genius for providing wise leaders who understood the needs of a new, democratic country. Under the Articles of Confederation, Virginia could not give the United States that leadership, however. Not until the Constitution was adopted in 1789 were Virginians able to fulfill this need, upon which America's very existence depended. Four of the first six Presidents of the United States under the Constitution—George Washington, Thomas Jefferson, James Madison, and James Monroe—were natives of Virginia. The other two, John Adams and his son, John Quincy Adams, came from Massachusetts. Founded in 1620, it, too, had become mature enough to give the nation great men to be leaders.

The third fundamental weakness under the Articles of Confederation was the inability of Congress to enforce its bills, even when they had been approved by nine states and had become the law of the United States. There was no way to force a state that balked to comply with the will of the majority. No machinery for this purpose existed. There were no political penalties, such as that of depriving the state's Congressional delegation of its seats until the state obeyed the law. There were also no financial penalties such as the automatic application of an economic boycott against the state.

The nation was so weak, in fact, that men everywhere

shrank from the very idea of punishing one of the thirteen states when it would not cooperate. The lack of a national army best illustrates that weakness. The small states and the states with few inhabitants were so afraid they might be dominated by their richer, more populous neighbors that they banded together and refused to authorize the formation of a national army.

Their fear was based on their long experience as colonies of a powerful nation. So their attitude, although not logical, was understandable. Nevertheless the interests of all Americans suffered.

The peace treaty signed in Paris in 1783 clearly established the physical boundaries of the United States. But since the new nation had no troops to guard her borders, Great Britain ignored the treaty and sent her own regiments to occupy the frontier forts in the wilderness. Similarly, the Indians of the interior knew there would be no organized reprisals against them, and felt free to attack settlers who moved into their hunting grounds.

The war-weary Americans who recognized these flaws in their new government could not feel great concern over them, however. Peace had seemed far away in 1781. Then, suddenly, the situation changed drastically when General Washington, leading a combined corps of American and French troops, and aided by the French fleet, won an overwhelming victory at Yorktown, Virginia. Great Britain was stunned by the defeat of her best troops, commanded by the able General Lord Cornwallis, and the government was forced to resign.

The new government, led by men sympathetic to the

cause of American liberty, publicly promised to open negotiations with the United States. The war had not yet ended, but eventual peace and freedom for the new nation were assured. In the meantime, General Sir Henry Clinton, the British commander in chief in the New World, continued to occupy New York. A British garrison still held Charleston, too, although that city was evacuated in 1782, when fighting still continued in South Carolina and Georgia.

Most states felt they could relax now, and their militia were called home and demobilized. And since many of the states were reluctant to support what they considered a large Continental Army, the new Congress was forced to suffer the humiliation of seeing some of its veteran regiments disbanded.

One more issue made the existence of the Confederation precarious. Eight of the thirteen states—New Hampshire, Massachusetts, Connecticut, New York, Virginia, North and South Carolina, and Georgia—claimed lands west of the Appalachian Mountains. These areas, the eight said, belonged to them because such rights were specified in the original charters granted to them as colonies by the British. The other five states—Pennsylvania, New Jersey, Delaware, Maryland, and Rhode Island—had specific boundaries, and therefore could make no similar claims.

Enterprising men in the five states had formed land companies within these areas during the 1760's. They had made treaties of their own with the Indian tribes of the region, and in scores of other ways had tried to strengthen their positions. These efforts had been resisted by the land-claiming states, led by the very able Virginia. The issue remained unsettled throughout the period of the Confederation. Battles were fought in Congress and elsewhere. With eight states ranged on one side and five on the other, neither side could achieve a nine-vote majority in the Congress. Often the work of the nation's representatives was paralyzed by the dispute, and more than once the country was on the verge of collapse because of the argument.

There were international repercussions as well; they brought the United States close to war with Spain (which controlled the Mississippi River and lands west of it) and intensified the domestic ill feeling. The landless states believed Spain would honor the claims of their citizens' private companies. Their representatives worked in Congress for the passage of a resolution assuring Spain that the United States did not want this territory. The eight states with claims to the area fought the resolution, and debates on the subject were endless.

John Jay of New York, the American Secretary of Foreign Affairs, became convinced that the stand of the five was sensible. He tried to make a treaty with Spain that relinquished American claims to the land. That effort rocked the infant United States to its insecure foundations. Such prominent financiers as Robert Morris of Philadelphia and others who were major shareholders in the landless states' private companies used economic pressure to bring down their foes. They did not succeed, but the bitterness on both sides became more intense.

The peace treaty created another domestic uproar in the United States that complicated American existence during the Confederation years. Commercial interests in England and Scotland pressed the British government to obtain guarantees that their prewar loans would be repaid. Most of the debtors were prominent Southern planters who, of course, wanted to be relieved of such repayments.

But the American commissioners who negotiated the treaty were in complete accord with the British on the matter. All three, as it happened, came from commercial centers that would benefit from a return to normal trade relations. John Adams was a Bostonian, John Jay was a New Yorker, and the venerable Benjamin Franklin was a Philadelphian. So, by accident rather than design, the principal cities of the United States were represented on the commission.

A clause to the effect that neither the United States nor Great Britain would interfere with the lawful collection of prewar debts was incorporated in the peace treaty. Members of nine state delegations voted in favor of the clause; they constituted a majority, and the clause was ratified. But four states—Virginia, North Carolina, South Carolina, and Georgia—were furious. Their planters never forgave the other states, and throughout the years of the Confederation, meetings of Congress were forced to listen to ringing Southern denunciations, no matter how urgent other government business may have been.

On paper, at least, the nine had won. But there was no national judiciary strong enough to enforce the collection of the debts, and the courts in the Southern states refused to order the planters to repay them. British and Scottish merchants who were unable to obtain their money refused to do business with other Americans. Businessmen in London and Edinburgh could not understand that the government of the Confederation was too feeble to compel its citizens to fulfill the obligations of the peace treaty.

The outraged merchants, traders, and shippers of the North retaliated by refusing to deal with the Southern planters. The hard feelings on both sides created deeprooted suspicions that lasted for three quarters of a century. This lack of understanding between North and South rightly may be regarded as one of the earliest causes of the American Civil War. Northern businessmen and Southern planters alike felt they had good reason to believe they had been injured by compatriots.

In spite of the tensions and troubles of the Confederation era, the United States survived. When the Constitution was written and adopted, Americans benefited from their errors and moved decisively to change their ways. Equally important, the states discovered that the United States would destroy herself if they did not work together, at least in some areas. The real miracle of the Confederation was that Americans were able to profit from mistakes that might have made a mockery of their long fight for freedom.

II. Radicals and Conservatives

For the better part of two hundred years it has been a convenient myth to think of the leaders of the American patriots—the rebels who broke away from England, who conducted and financed the Revolution, and subsequently governed the new nation—as a closely united group. According to this legend, there was no break in this solid structure until, during the first Administration of President Washington after the adoption of the Constitution, the conflicting political philosophies of Thomas Jefferson and Alexander Hamilton began to clash. Nothing could be further from the truth.

The dispute between Jefferson and Hamilton did occur, of course, and out of it grew the two-party system in American politics that, with minor variations, has persisted down to the present day. Perhaps the absence of formal political parties prior to their great confrontation is responsible for the myth. But the facts of the matter are plain: There were two very different approaches to the basic concept of American government since the time that colonial leaders first began to think and speak of establishing their own nation.

Sam Adams, whose propaganda inflamed American public opinion in the days preceding the Revolution, was considered a disreputable radical by most of his fellow patriot leaders. Many disapproved of the way he exaggerated a minor fight with British troops in Boston and called it the "Boston Massacre." They, like Adams, advocated the refusal of Americans to pay taxes on tea and other products, which the British government demanded as symbols of Crown authority; but they were dismayed when Adams resorted to force and a group of his followers dumped large quantities of British tea into Boston Harbor.

The individual's financial status did not necessarily determine his position in the so-called radical or conservative groups. One of Adams' first and most prominent disciples was John Hancock, who owned the largest fleet of merchant ships and the most extensive warehouses of any man in the colonies. Patrick Henry of Virginia developed a similar brand of radicalism. It is significant that Henry preferred to serve as Governor of Virginia to accepting posts as United States Secretary of State or Chief Justice of the Supreme Court. During the few periods of his adult life that he did not hold public office, Henry was a successful attorney, although he did not become wealthy until his later years.

Jefferson, who eventually owned large farming properties, was a radical from his youth. James Madison of Virginia, who was close to Jefferson, was far more conservative. The one prominent American who refused to stand with either side was General Washington. During his Presidency, however, the conservatives—by then led by Hamilton—gained the upper hand.

One of the earliest conservatives was Robert Morris, the Philadelphia financier. John Adams became identified with the group, as did Richard Henry Lee of Virginia, the single most prominent member of the Congress for a decade. Benjamin Franklin, the country's most important diplomat, was in Europe throughout much of the war and thereafter, but he quietly used his influence in favor of the conservative cause.

By the time the Declaration of Independence was signed, the vague radicalism of one faction and the equally amorphous conservatism of the other had begun to take specific form. The war was under way. This disposed of all questions concerning the means that Americans should use to work toward freedom. The advocates of caution had lost. The will of the radicals had prevailed, and the issue would be settled by force of arms. The Declaration of Independence, written in the main by Jefferson, with sage advice from Lee and Franklin, among others, had put the final seal on the matter.

Now a new and urgent question arose. What form would the new government of the United States take? The radicals felt a deep lack of trust in a strong central government of any kind. Such a government, they felt, would be similar in many ways to that of Great Britain. Therefore, they believed, such a government would place the liberty of the individual in jeopardy. Their experience with Great Britain dictated their position. They felt as they did because they feared that what had happened to them in the past might happen again, even though the new government would be made up only of Americans.

The conservatives, on the other hand, believed with equal conviction that the new nation could survive and prosper only if her affairs were administered by a national government. Morris and others were aware of the chaos that already existed, thanks to the right kept by each state to issue its own money. All financial policies, Morris felt, should be directed by one office, that of a national treasurer.

A single policy on foreign affairs was essential, Benjamin Franklin declared. It would be madness if each of the thirteen states developed its own approach to dealings with other nations. Furthermore, he said, the very nature of diplomatic relations was delicate. For this reason, diplomacy was usually practiced in secret, and it would be catastrophic if everything concerning the relations of the United States with other nations were subject to open debate on the floor of the Congress. A ministry of foreign affairs should conduct these relations.

The radicals, who had virtually no experience in foreign affairs, loudly disagreed with Franklin. The new nation had nothing to hide, they said. Only tyrants who wanted to curb liberty had to deal with others in secret. The free and independent United States would best preserve her freedoms if everything relating to her foreign relations were brought into the open.

The question of military operations also split the two groups. When General Washington accepted the command of the new Continental Army, he made it plain that the conduct of warfare required the control of operations by a single, national command. The radicals were afraid to fight Washington in the open, as he was virtually the only man in whom all Americans had faith as a military leader. But these advocates of "open dealings" themselves engaged in some private maneuvers.

The militia of each state, they believed, had the right to operate independently, and so they resisted all efforts to place these militia units under General Washington's direct command. From the morning of April 19, 1775, when the first shots of the Revolution were fired in Lexington, Massachusetts, until the signing of the peace treaty in 1783, the militia remained independent of the Continental Army.

This separation was essential, such men as Sam Adams and Patrick Henry contended. "The militia," Henry declared in a typical fiery speech, "provide Americans with a warranty that tyranny will not sink roots in our free soil."

The militia of the individual states were responsible for the worst American battle losses of the war. Ill-trained, undisciplined, and poorly armed, these units fled from combat more often than they stood in battle and fought. The Continentals felt contempt for their part-time soldier comrades, and even militia officers admitted their troops were inferior. But the civilian champions of the militia could not be budged.

John Jay of New York, among others who were thinking in long-range terms, believed that the executive management of the nation made a central government necessary. Then, he said, men would grow familiar with their positions and their experience would enable them to guide the country successfully for relatively long periods.

But the radicals were afraid that an officeholder would grow accustomed to power. He might resort to tyrannical means to prevent someone else from taking his place.

Delegates to the Continental Congress from virtually all states were elected for periods of only one year. These delegates served on Congressional committees that supervised, to a very limited extent, the coordination of the states' activities. This was true in every field of endeavor from crop growing to mail delivery to the encouragement of international trade.

"A member of the Congress who may not be returned to office by his electorate at the end of a given year," Patrick Henry said, "has little chance to acquire the tastes of a tyrant."

"That same Congressional committee member," Robert Morris replied, "has too short a time to learn the needs of the people, so he is unable to discharge his obligations to them."

By 1776, the former radicals had become the firm advocates of the rights of the separate individual states, and the opponents of a national government. The conservatives had become the champions of national government and wanted to cut down the powers of the states.

Specific issues caused many individual delegates to the Congress to hold conflicting views. As has been noted earlier, the states'-rights men believed in unit rule in the Congress. In other words, they wanted each state delegation to have one vote, and to vote in all matters as a unit. The advocates of a strong national government, on the other hand, believed in proportional representation. They felt that a delegation's size should depend on its population, and that members should vote as individuals.

Most delegates from the more heavily populated states —Massachusetts, New York, Pennsylvania, and Virginia— wanted proportional representation. But most delegates from the nine other states, a majority in the Congress, insisted there be no change in the rule that maintained the power of the separate states.

The case of Patrick Henry illustrates the complex character and seeming inconsistency of an individual. A fierce, lifelong champion of states' rights and a foe of national government, Henry, as a Virginian, favored proportional representation, which would have given Virginia greater power in the government.

In 1776, a committee of the Continental Congress was elected by the Congress to draw up the Articles of Confederation, America's first constitution. The chairman, who wrote most of the document himself, seemed uniquely qualified for the post.

Maryland-born John Dickinson, as a boy had moved to Delaware, at a time when it was a part of Pennsylvania. The political situation in Pennsylvania and Delaware was unique: Until the outbreak of the war, the Crown-appointed Governor of Pennsylvania also served as Governor of Delaware.

Dickinson moved back and forth between towns in Delaware and Pennsylvania. Throughout his entire adult life he had business interests and strong personal friendships in both states. Therefore, although elected to the Continental Congress from Delaware, he also had a great deal of sympathy for Pennsylvania's large-state point of view.

One of the few patriots opposed to the Declaration of Independence, Dickinson lost much popularity because of that stand. A moderate, reasonable man, he wanted independence, but believed it could best be achieved through negotiations with the British government rather than through a war that was certain to be fought to the end when the United States would thumb her nose at the mother country. Nevertheless, no man served the American cause more faithfully than Dickinson after the Declaration was issued. Known as "the pamphleteer of the Revolution," he wrote and published countless documents throughout the war. His pamphlets' influence in encouraging Americans to continue the struggle was immeasurable.

Dickinson's greatest strength was his ability to see every side of a question. In fact, many of his colleagues thought he was too reasonable. He tried to satisfy the demands of both the states'-rights men and the strong-national-government men—with the result of pleasing neither. He and his committee completed work on the Articles of Confederation at the same time the Declaration of Independence was issued.

He presented the Articles to the Congress early in July, and created a deadlock that could not be broken for thirteen years! The Continental Congress debated the Articles until 1781, when they were adopted in a form that favored the states'-rights group. But the issue was not really resolved until the Constitution of 1787 was adopted in 1789. That great document, made up of many compromises, favored a strong national government.

Precisely where Dickinson himself stood throughout the war and the Confederation period has been a matter of endless debate. Through the years, historians have disagreed on this point. By 1787, however, Dickinson clearly saw the faults of a government that gave basic powers to the states instead of serving as the government of all the people. He was a delegate to the Constitutional Convention, and his influence in both Delaware and Pennsylvania was so great that they were the first two states to ratify it.

In 1776, however, no man could achieve the impossible. Neither the states'-rights nor the national-government champions would accept compromise. Only after suffering from their mistakes would the people of the United States and their elected representatives be willing to form a democratic government that could function.

John Dickinson's draft of the Articles of Confederation was the subject of violent debate in the Continental Congress from early July, 1776, until the middle of the following month. Members were so incensed that they neglected issues of immediate concern in the prosecution of the war and instead spent hours arguing over the Articles.

The first issue that caused an explosion was that of lands west of the Appalachian Mountains. On this issue Dickinson stood with the landless states. As it happened, their selfish interests coincided with those of men who wanted a powerful central government. The Dickinson clause gave the Congress the right to establish all boundaries between the mountains and the Mississippi River.

In a sense, the question was academic. Only a few American settlers had moved into the area, which was also claimed by Great Britain and by Spain. But the eight states with claims to land in the region were alarmed. The Articles of Confederation offered them no assurances their property would not be taken from them and eventually made into new, separate states. They were horrified and demanded an ironclad guarantee that the boundaries they claimed would not be altered.

The issue of representation created another storm. Dickinson took a basic stand with the states'-rights men. His draft of the Articles provided that each state be granted one unit vote in the Congress. At the same time, however, he saw the justice of the demands being made for proportional representation. So his draft recognized the importance of these demands and hinted that a compromise might be found.

The compromise Dickinson suggested was incorporated into the Constitution of 1787. That document provided for two houses of Congress. The demands of the states'-rights men were met in the creation of the Senate, made up of two members from each state. The demands of the proportional-representation men were met in the creation of the House of Representatives, where membership is based on each state's population.

The greatest outcry in the debate of 1776 was raised over the "internal police" article. Complete control of internal police functions was specifically granted to the separate states. The logical Dickinson assumed that if each state controlled its own police, the national government would not be able to create a police force that might destroy the personal liberties of the people.

The states'-rights men did not argue about their right to establish and maintain their own police forces. They took such a right for granted. They were offended because the article mentioned *only* this right. Unscrupulous men who held office in the central government, they argued, might usurp scores of other rights that were not specifically set out in detail in the article.

The work of the Continental Congress was paralyzed by the debate. So many matters directly connected with the war required their immediate attention that discussion of the Articles was postponed. Feelings ran so high, however, that many members insisted the debate continue. Three days of argument on the subject of whether to put off the argument followed before a majority, representing nine states, voted to table the Articles.

In April, 1777, the Continental Congress resumed the debate. The United States was losing the war, delegates were forced to deal realistically with the matter, and there was quick agreement on all questions that were not controversial. The majority, representing the states'-rights view, urged that the debated articles be rewritten.

This was easier said than done. The British commander in chief, General Sir William Howe, had other plans. He had taken New York the previous year and made it his principal base. Now he wanted to capture Philadelphia, the American capital. He believed its fall might end the war.

General Washington's inadequately equipped Continentals and undisciplined militia fought a series of holding actions, losing each of these battles. The Congress, forced to deal with immediate matters while it nervously watched the campaign, again postponed a discussion of the Articles.

In September, General Howe's Redcoats swept into Philadelphia. The Congress did not surrender, however, as the British had hoped. Instead they traveled into the remote hills of Pennsylvania and established the temporary capital of the United States of America in the little town of York. There the Articles were revised according to the will of the majority.

Since nine states approved the single-vote-per-state rule, it was adopted. No majority could be obtained on the question of the lands beyond the Appalachians, so nothing was done. For a time the debate on this issue became so bitter that the Congress was almost disrupted. Then men of good sense on both sides curbed the hotheads. The subject was shelved.

Delegate Thomas Burke of North Carolina proposed a new article to replace that dealing with internal police. Instead of granting police powers to the states, he wrote an amendment vesting *all* sovereign power in the states except those very limited powers specifically granted to the Congress. The states'-rights advocates mustered an overwhelming majority in favor of this amendment, and the vote was so one-sided there was no real contest.

In November, 1777, work on the Articles of Confederation was completed by the Continental Congress. Under the rules passed by the Congress, unanimous ratification was necessary in order to create the government proposed under the Articles.

Within less than a year, twelve of the thirteen states ratified the Articles. It is remarkable that the state legislatures acted so quickly. The nation was fighting for survival, and men had to travel great distances to attend the sessions of the legislatures. Living, as they did, in an age when it was difficult to communicate even by mail, they were forced to schedule their sessions far in advance.

The desire of men in every part of the nation for a stable, permanent government was so great that the legislatures spent little time debating the details of the Articles. They preferred to vote in favor of ratification, hoping that conditions would improve.

One state, however, refused to ratify the Articles until, as a resolution passed by its legislature stated, "a grave injustice" was corrected. "For the good of the whole," Maryland demanded, control of the West should be given to the Continental Congress. The resolution made one exception: All land claims granted in the West prior to the Declaration of Independence were to be honored. In other words, Maryland wanted to make certain that the land companies formed by some of her prominent citizens would retain their holdings.

Virginia struck back furiously. Her legislature promptly declared void all private claims in her territory beyond the mountains.

Maryland took her case to the Congress. There her delegates argued that the cause of the nation was more important than that of any one selfish state.

By now, in 1778 and 1779, the repercussions of the

Battle of Saratoga were being felt. And General Washington's corps had become a disciplined, hard-bitten force of professional soldiers after suffering the agonies of the 1777–78 winter in the raw countryside at Valley Forge, Pennsylvania. The French treaty of alliance had gone into effect, and supplies, ammunition, and troops were being landed in the New World. The presence of a French fleet of warships off the American coast encouraged the owners of merchantmen to resume their lucrative trade in the West Indies.

Spain, the ally of France and the neighbor of the United States in the Floridas and lands west of the Mississippi, indicated that she might be willing to negotiate a treaty of recognition with the new nation. Meanwhile she was willing to permit her colonies to trade with the Americans.

The harvests in 1778 and 1779 were good, and in all thirteen states there was enough to eat for the first time in years. There was a dramatic increase in the number of volunteers joining the Continental Army.

So Americans finally could cling to more than a remote hope that they might be able to win their independence in the distant future. It was possible that the day was drawing closer more rapidly than even the most optimistic had allowed themselves to believe. Massachusetts, Pennsylvania, and New York began to press Virginia to cede her lands to the United States. So did some of the less powerful smaller states. Two notable exceptions were Connecticut and North Carolina, which had important claims of their own. Neither, however, was being pushed by her sister states.

New York set an example for Virginia by ceding her own lands to the nation as a whole. It did not matter that the New York claims were relatively weak, or that her principal city was under occupation, crippling her. The gesture was important for its own sake.

Virginia became increasingly unpopular with the other states. Charges that she lacked patriotism were unfair, but her leaders could not help feeling hurt by them. They worked out a careful bill of cession designed to quiet the storm. Virginia's legislature agreed, and passed the bill. The state's territories in the West were ceded to the United States *provided* that the Congress declared void all deeds given to private companies or individuals by Indian tribes.

For all practical purposes, this provision made the act of cession little more than an empty gesture. It guaranteed that Virginia and the other seven states with land claims would not agree to any such declaration by the Congress. The five landless states, as usual, would be outnumbered.

Nevertheless, Virginia had gone through the motions of complying with the request, and her sister states— particularly her land-claiming friends—had no intention of examining the move critically. The situations of Virginia and Maryland were suddenly and dramatically reversed.

By now it was the end of 1780; a most difficult year it had been. The lack of a permanent government was hampering the new nation's ability to prosecute the war, to establish diplomatic relations with other countries, and to put her tangled financial affairs in order. The states banded together to demand that Maryland accept the Virginia act of cession. In vain the Maryland delegates to the Congress argued that what Virginia had done lacked meaning. They were reminded that there was a need for Maryland, too, to act for "the good of the whole."

Unable to resist the pressures, the Maryland legislature ratified the Articles of Confederation on March 1, 1781. After five and a half years of makeshift administrations, the United States finally had a national government. Since that government had a sound legal foundation, the American bankers and merchants had cause to hope that large sums of money might be borrowed abroad. It was possible that some foreign governments, perhaps France, Spain, or some of the wealthier German principalities, might make the United States a long-term loan.

The formation of a new, permanent government was received with great pleasure in Philadelphia, which had been reestablished as the American capital following the evacuation of Howe's successor, General Sir Henry Clinton. The event was celebrated on March 3. General Henry Knox's artillery boomed, and a parade by infantry and cavalry was witnessed by most of the city's people. The new Continental Navy took part, too. The *Ariel*, a frigate commanded by Captain John Paul Jones, fired its guns, and that night was decorated with lights for the occasion.

A formal reception was held by the Congress at two o'clock in the afternoon, with foreign diplomats and military advisers in attendance. A banquet was served to the guests and demonstrated that America's days of famine had come to an end. The main dish was wild boar, but those who did not care for it had a wide variety of choices. Thousands of raw oysters were served, hams and turkeys were carved, and five different kinds of fish were grilled. There were ample desserts, too— cakes, tarts, pastries, and pies. The guests drank French wines as well as native ale and mead. Whisky was served, as well as Dutch gin and West Indian rum.

After dark, a huge fireworks display was presented for the entertainment of the entire population of Philadelphia. Although the night was very cold, a Continental Army fife-and-drum corps gave a concert that lasted more than three hours.

The festivities were so jolly that most men, the members of the Congress included, momentarily allowed themselves to forget that the war had not yet been won. Nor did they choose to remember that the financial difficulties the United States faced appeared virtually insurmountable.

Robert Morris and his fellow bankers remained aware of the critical situation, however, as did the wealthy men in other states. They had been financing the war out of their own pockets, receiving notes from the Continental Congress in return. No one knew better than they that the notes were worthless.

They hoped, desperately, that the new Continental Congress would be able to solve the problem. If it could not, the bankers would be destroyed. And the nation itself, even if it won the war, might perish.

III. Economic Problems
in the New Nation

Only the South, where Generals Nathanael Greene, Anthony Wayne, and Francis Marion led Americans Continentals and militia, remained active as a theater of war after Washington's victory at Yorktown in October, 1781. Elsewhere, with the encouragement of the Continental Congress, troops were demobilized and went home.

The rapid dismemberment of the military force it had taken the United States six and a half years of toil to create appears senseless at first glance. Although the fighting had diminished, it had not yet stopped. The British were afraid they would lose prestige if they withdrew from Charleston and the chain of forts they still held in South Carolina and Georgia. They were determined to hold these posts, and the Americans were just as determined to expel them.

The situation of Sir Henry Clinton in New York was

somewhat different. He continued to command a large number of first-rate troops, who were protected by a powerful Royal Navy fleet. So an operation to dislodge him would have been bloody and expensive, a waste of lives and of money.

Clinton's continued presence in New York was not a stubborn or vengeful quirk. Officially, the British still regarded their New World foes as rebels. The granting of recognition to the new nation was a solemn matter, complicated by the need to settle scores of legal, financial, and humanitarian issues. For example: Would the Continental Congress grant amnesties to those Americans who had remained loyal to the Crown? What disposition would be made of Crown property in the United States? Would British subjects who had been dispossessed from their American homes be paid an equitable sum for their property?

Both sides expected hard bargaining on these and many other matters. So the British government reasoned that by keeping Clinton in New York they would prevent the victory-flushed Americans from making too many unreasonable demands. No one on either side expected a resumption of major hostilities, however. Therefore the Americans saw no need to keep a large force in uniform to prevent Clinton from starting a new campaign. Everyone expected the peace commissioners to hammer out an agreement both sides could accept. If they failed, it would be time enough to recall Washington's veterans to contain Sir Henry's regiments and, if necessary, drive them out of the country.

The rapid demobilization of troops that took place in the late autumn of 1781 and the winter months of 1781–82 set a precedent the United States has followed in every subsequent war. When the fighting ends, the troops go home and return to civilian life. The attitudes of eighteenth-century Americans have shaped the thinking and policy decisions of the nation for the past two hundred years.

In a word, the Founding Fathers of the United States did not trust professional soldiers and regarded a standing army as an evil. Professional soldiers made them suspicious and uneasy, in the same way they thought of professional politicians holding office in a central government as threats to their liberties. "It is our peculiar genius as a people," Thomas Jefferson wrote a few years later, "to be a nation of amateurs. Our political and diplomatic officials hold their places for a few years and then return to private life, giving way to others."

Patrick Henry expressed the feelings of most Americans in a letter he sent to Washington soon after the commander in chief retired to his estate in Virginia. "The nation is in your debt, sir," he wrote. "You not only led our farmers and townsmen to victory in battle, but you have set an example for our generals and colonels. Did your excellency but wish it, you could persuade our citizens to make you their king. But you have laid aside your uniform to become, once again, a simple planter. May the fortune you so tragically lost due to the selflessness of your service be restored to you."

John Hancock put matters more bluntly. "Scratch a

general," he wrote to his young friend Aaron Burr, "and you will find a tyrant. I am relieved that Washington has been persuaded to lay down his sword."

Hancock revealed an unfair bias, to be sure. As jealous as he was competent and patriotic, he resented Washington's popularity with the people. He and the other civilians, he believed, had contributed more to victory than had the commander in chief. Actually, no one had "persuaded" General Washington to retire from the command of the Continental Army. His private affairs had been neglected since he had first donned his uniform in April, 1775. He was not only heartily sick of war, but needed to repair his estate.

John Hancock was far from being alone, however, in believing that high-ranking officers might want to become dictators and deprive the people of the liberties they had fought so hard to win. John Adams of Massachusetts, who would become the first Vice President and second President of the United States after the adoption of the Constitution in 1789, wrote to Major General Horatio Gates, "We don't choose to trust you generals, with too much power, for too long a time."

There was ample cause for mistrust on both sides. The Army had been overbearing in its attitude toward the Continental Congress, and the civilians felt they had been subjected to exorbitant demands. Former officers and enlisted men were already agitating for pensions in 1783, and there was a concerted movement under way to obtain half-pay for life.

Public sentiment favored such payments. The soldiers, after all, had beaten the Redcoats. And in return they had suffered extraordinary hardships. For the better part of the war they had been underfed, and often had starved. Until the French had sent quantities of cloth in the final year or two of combat, virtually no one had been uniformed. The man who had owned a pair of boots with whole soles had considered himself fortunate. The troops of every rank had been paid their wages in worthless paper money issued by Congress, and one of the most popular of slang expressions in the country was that something without value wasn't "worth a Continental," as this money was called.

Many members of the new Continental Congress privately sympathized with the veterans, but they felt their own hands were tied. They were willing to reward the conquerors with pensions, but had no funds for the purpose and no known sources of revenue. John Jay of New York put the matter succinctly: "No one wants to deprive a veteran of his due, but where will we find the silver and gold to line his purse? Let him tell the new Congress where to find a treasure, and he will be paid. If he chooses to do nothing but complain, however, he will avail himself nothing. Congressmen are not alchemists, and we have at hand only dross."

The demand of the veterans for half-pay made some politicians fear that the former soldiers might try to achieve their ends by illegally seizing control of the government. But most members of Congress, along with the nation's bankers and other men of means, realized that the question was just a symptom of a far larger problem. Perhaps the greatest dilemma facing the infant United States was that of becoming financially solvent.

The troops of the Continental Army had not been the only people who had been given useless paper money. In all, the Continental Congress had printed approximately $250 million worth of scrip. Neither gold nor any other precious metal had supported any of this issue. In fact, as banker Robert Morris of Philadelphia said, "Only our prayers for freedom offered security for our foolish Continental dollars."

Twelve of the thirteen states also had issued paper money of their own, and a number had manufactured coins as well. Only Georgia had refrained, but its citizens could not congratulate themselves. They had wanted to print money, but there were no presses in their tiny frontier villages. Nevertheless, Georgia alone had escaped hopeless debt. Elsewhere, businessmen, property owners, and other citizens of substance who had accumulated large quantities of Continental and state paper money were clamoring for real funds they could use to pay off their own creditors.

Farmers who had sold food supplies to the Continental Army and the militia of the states had a legitimate complaint of their own. Ever since 1775, they had provided literally millions of tons worth of grain, cheese, meat, and other foodstuffs. In return they had received what were known as "quartermaster receipts." In other words, the Army officers in charge of obtaining supplies had written I.O.U.'s promising that the Continental Congress would pay for the food at the end of the war.

Now, of course, the farmers wanted to collect. They had shown their patriotism and had made sacrifices; their demands were just. Each month sheaves of I.O.U.'s flooded Congress. By June, 1784, more than a hundred million dollars' worth of these demands had been received. They continued to pour in, but no accurate records indicate the total amount. Apparently the financiers of Congress were so frustrated they did not try to add up the total.

These unpaid bills caused inflation, and food prices mounted at an alarming rate. For example, a five-pound loaf of bread had cost a halfpenny in Boston at the start of the war in 1775. In the autumn of 1783, a two-pound loaf cost three pennies—when it was available. Some days the bakeries had no flour on hand and were forced to close their doors.

There were shortages everywhere. For several months in late 1783, it was impossible to buy chickens and other poultry in Philadelphia. When the Redcoats evacuated Charleston in 1782, the city clamored for salt. There were no spare supplies in the entire country large enough to meet Charleston's demand, and her citizens rioted. Brigadier General Francis Marion, Charleston's greatest war hero, was forced to make a journey to the city from the interior, where he was harassing the British troops that still infested South Carolina and Georgia. Not until he threatened martial law was order restored.

Nowhere in the United States was there enough cornmeal, coffee, or sugar. To say the least, this situation was ironic. The owners of merchant ships were resuming trade with the West Indian islands on a large scale and were obtaining ample supplies of coffee and molasses. But they would not sell them on credit, nor would they barter them. They wanted cash, and since none was available, they preferred to store these supplies until conditions improved.

John Hancock's huge warehouses in Boston were empty at the end of the war, but within six months they were overflowing. The coffee and sugar stored there were worth such a huge fortune that he hired a number of war veterans to guard his property. He was wise. The demand for sugar and coffee was so great that the people of Boston might have been tempted to break in and steal what they wanted. But the guards deterred them.

The shortage of cornmeal in the cities and towns of the United States was absurd. Never before had so much grain been grown in the country. The weather in the spring and summer of 1783 was perfect. Returning soldiers joined their fathers and brothers on the farms, so there was, at long last, ample manpower to grow and harvest crops.

But the farmers kept their supplies for themselves. Bags of dried corn were piled high in thousands of cellars. The farmers had learned a lesson, and refused to part with their grain unless they received hard cash in return. They would let the corn rot, they said, rather than accept worthless paper money for it.

The shelves of grocers, butchers, and fishmongers in the cities and towns often were bare. Yet America, more than ever before, was a land of plenty. There were fish in the rivers, lakes, and sea. The forests abounded with game. Cattle, hogs, and poultry flourished. Corn and wheat grew high, and apples, peaches, pears, and other fruit were plump in the orchards.

It is small wonder that city and country dwellers soon came to hate one another. The mutual lack of trust that developed during the early years of the Confedcration persisted down to the twentieth century, long after the nation had expanded across the continent to the Pacific Ocean.

"Only a wizard or necromancer," Robert Morris said wearily, "is capable of solving an insoluble problem. Congress cannot."

Funds were needed to make the economy function, and there were two obvious sources. The first one was the wealthy citizens who had carried most of the war's financial burden. Naturally, they were reluctant to part with the cash that remained in their dwindling fortunes.

The other potential source was the foreign investor, be it a government or a private banker or merchant. Here, again, the Confederation faced grave difficulties. France had loaned the United States more than ten million dollars in gold during the final years of the war. Neither her government nor her wealthy individuals were interested in putting up more money until the previous debt was repaid. Spain had supplied more than a million dollars, and felt the same way.

Great Britain turned a deaf ear to hints from her former colonies that investments would be welcome. In fact, British merchants and bankers were going to law courts in the hope to recover their lost properties, the land and houses and wharves that Americans had seized at the beginning of the war.

The Continental Congress had no authority to take

strong measures in order to create a new, healthy situation. It could only advise, and this it did. Individual states were urged to stop printing paper money. "The state that confines its new money to coin is the prudent state," a Congressional memorandum declared.

The states took the hint. As previously issued paper money came into state treasuries, it was turned over to Congress; a special committee of Congressmen solemnly burned it. As a rule, the states acquired this money in one way: They sold state lands to individuals, accepting scrip in return.

The Continental Congress followed the same policy, selling national lands in return for the almost worthless Continental dollars. This money also was burned by the busy committee.

It is significant that land was the one commodity that had real value. Even in Massachusetts, New York, and Pennsylvania, the most heavily populated states, there were huge tracts of wilderness lands. The soil was rich, the timber stands were themselves worth fortunes to anyone with a willingness and energy to cut and trim the trees. "Our land," said Thomas Jefferson, "is our one viable commodity. It is the hope that we will become a prosperous agricultural nation that keeps our nation together in these trying times. It is the knowledge that we have the ability to become a wealthy nation devoted to peace that gives us the courage to face our trials of the present."

Gradually the policy of "retiring" the paper money had an effect. By 1785, the inflation had been checked.

The trend had not been reversed, and prices were still very high, but people could console themselves with the thought that affairs were no longer going from bad to worse.

The quartermaster certificates held by the farmers remained a bone of contention, however. The Continental Congress had no ready cash to pay off these debts. Some Congressmen questioned the validity of the certificates, and the farmers were furious, saying their honesty was being disputed.

This issue dragged on through the entire period of the Confederation; long after the Constitution was adopted, farmers and the government bickered and fought. The last claims were not settled until the late 1790's, during the Administration of President John Adams.

"Land is saving us from ruin," Alexander Hamilton of New York wrote in 1784. "It is a pity that the Confederation and the states cannot arouse the interest of the farmers in additional property holdings."

The farmers, of course, were finding their present property holdings something of a burden. They had more than enough to eat, but, like everyone else, they were short of cash. Still, they were more fortunate than the city dwellers, who often went hungry. As a direct result of the lack of adequate food supplies in the cities and towns, people migrated by the thousands and tens of thousands to the frontier, where land was available either without cost or for a nominal sum.

The bankers, among them Robert Morris, realized

there would be an enormous boom in land during years to come, and bought all they could. Other men of substance joined them, and a new evil was created. Land companies were formed, and men interested in making a quick return on their investments sometimes overextended themselves.

A crash was inevitable. Some of the land companies were such flimsy ventures that they collapsed of their own weight. Prominent citizens were bankrupted overnight and were forced to endure the humiliation of spending terms in debtors' prisons. Morris was such a victim, as was Colonel Light-Horse Harry Lee of Virginia, the great cavalry hero of the Revolution.

Nevertheless, it was the land that enabled the new nation to survive the period of the weak Confederation. Shrewd bankers and financiers in Holland recognized the worth of making long-range investments in American property. No precise figures are available, but it is estimated that the thrifty Dutch spent more than ten million dollars in gold and silver for wilderness properties in the United States. John Jay said these funds saved the American economy from total collapse. And the benefit to the Dutch was enormous. Within fifty years, the land they had purchased was worth more than sixty million dollars.

Descendants of some of the Dutch investors moved to the United States, and many of the properties bought by their ancestors remain in the hands of their families to this day. Most are located in New York, Pennsylvania, and Delaware, and these real estate holdings are now even more valuable.

Certainly the Dutch investments were a great help, but the Continental Congress desperately needed money for its own treasury. "We cannot collect revenues through our customs agents," said Dr. Benjamin Rush of Pennsylvania, the distinguished physician-statesman-patriot, "unless we employ customs agents. Such agents must needs have the wherewithall to eat and house themselves, so we need silver that is not debased for to pay their wages."

The most obvious method of fund-raising was that of floating a national bond issue. The Continental Congress acted accordingly, and authorized such an issue; the public was offered bonds for fifty dollars that, in twenty-five years, would bring seventy-five dollars in return, and seventy-five-dollar bonds that would repay the purchaser one hundred dollars.

The same patriotic Americans, civilian and military, who had led the nation in war, responded to the call. George Washington and Benjamin Franklin bought bonds, as did John Adams, John Hancock, Caesar Rodney of Delaware, and Robert Livingston of New York. Robert Morris made substantial purchases, as did Gouverneur Morris, also of Pennsylvania but no relative. Alexander Hamilton made a substantial contribution, and so did Thomas Jefferson and James Madison.

These men were not philanthropists. The one hundred or more citizens who bought large quantities of the new government's bonds were not making contributions to charity. Many were sacrificing their own security, their own immediate financial comfort in order to help the Confederation. In fact, only Hancock and one or two others could afford a severe loss and still remain financially solvent.

Why, then, did they buy the bonds? The answer is simple. They believed with all their hearts in the United States and were confident of her future.

The failure of the Confederation placed their investments in grave jeopardy. When Robert Morris emerged from debtors' prison, for example, his only assets were his dubious Confederation bonds. If the United States survived and prospered, he would become wealthy again; if the young nation collapsed, he would, in all probability, return to debtors' prison.

An examination of this situation would not be complete without a few words on the theories of the late Dr. Charles A. Beard, the noted historian who was the twentieth century's most widely recognized expert on the early days of the United States. According to Dr. Beard, it was these bonds, held by a relatively small number of men, that led to the writing and adoption of the Constitution that is the basis for the present and enduring form of government in the United States.

The bonds, Dr. Beard said, would have become worthless had the Confederation continued beyond 1789. A stronger national government was needed to make them worth their face value. So it was the bondholders who called the Constitutional Convention in 1787, wrote a new Constitution that provided for an infinitely more powerful federal government, and worked successfully for the adoption of that Constitution.

For the better part of a half century, most authorities have accepted the ideas of Dr. Beard. Although no one really knows the motives of the Founding Fathers, their actions indicate that Dr. Beard was probably right.

So, in a sense, the weaknesses of the Confederation as well as its strengths contributed materially to its successive form of government, which has been called the most successful democracy ever established.

IV. The Greatest Asset

Although food in the cities and towns was scarce, there was no money, and the economic prospects of the infant United States seemed frightening, the people of the new nation were anything but frightened or downhearted. On the contrary, their faith in the future and their exuberant determination to create a new kind of civilization provided an inspiration to the poor and oppressed peoples of Europe.

"America," wrote Tom Paine, the fiery and gifted pamphleteer of the Revolution, "is the hope of tomorrow, the salvation, on this earth, of mankind."

"The Lord God Almighty," said the Reverend Isaiah Dimmock of New London, Connecticut, in a sermon on Thanksgiving Day, 1783, "has seen fit to bless this land as He has blessed no other."

"God has blessed our America and made of it a new, unique nation," said the Reverend Thomas Mandeville of Charleston, South Carolina, on the same occasion.

"The whole world," declared the Reverend Francis Thompson of Trenton, New Jersey, in a Thanksgiving

Day sermon, "has cause to envy the people of this bright land."

Everywhere, again and again, the same theme was heard: America is a bright land. The Pennsylvania *Gazette* and the Boston *Advertiser* said it repeatedly. The Fourth of July, Independence Day, became the most important holiday of the year, and speakers at celebrations in every city, town, and village stressed the same theme: The land is bright.

This optimism took many forms, but at no time was it emotional. The eighteenth-century Enlightenment, often called the Age of Reason, came late to the New World, but it did come. Calm reason and logic were admired; irrational outbursts were deplored. The most universally respected man in the United States was Dr. Benjamin Franklin of Philadelphia, who was a diplomat and scientist, an author and editor and publisher. But above all, he was a philosopher, and his countrymen looked up to him, as they looked up to Thomas Jefferson as a thinker.

Knowledge, American clergymen, editors, and educators said, was the only king. Monarchs like King George III, to whom the people of the United States no longer owed allegiance, belonged to the past, as did elaborate religious and other ceremonials. Therefore the American people had cause to rejoice, and rejoice they did.

They had formed the first "pure democracy" in the history of civilization, a democracy far superior to that of the ancient Greeks, who restricted voting privileges to men of certain classes. In the United States every freeman could become a citizen, and every freeman had a right to vote. Therefore, every freeman had an active voice in his government.

The nation dreamed of becoming perfect in all things. After all, her people felt, they had achieved their independence under miraculous conditions. In 1775, there had been few who had believed that freedom could be won. But the impossible had come true, and they now had their own nation, recognized by the world's leading powers.

They were well aware of their own national potential: the rich soil, the waterpower in the great rivers, the timber and furs and other natural resources.

Above all, there was land. The nation was expanding westward toward the Mississippi. The Kentucky district of Virginia had some of the finest soil and best forest lands on the entire continent. The Franklin district of North Carolina was agitating for separate statehood, which it would achieve in another decade and a half as Tennessee. It had some of the best potential waterpower sites in the whole country. The Ohio Valley was dazzling, and offered great promise to settlers. Kentucky and Massachusetts had land claims that stretched toward the Mississippi. And a few of the boldest Americans dreamed of the day when the nation would extend across the entire continent.

The new America, her people believed, would be unlike any other nation on earth. The principles of Jefferson's reason, as they had appeared in the Declaration of Independence, which he had written, would apply to everyone. All men were created equal. All men were endowed with certain unalienable rights, among them life, liberty, and the pursuit of happiness.

These lofty expressions were not mere ideals. They were attainable, within the grasp of every American, then and there. The arts and sciences would be fostered. Crops would be grown according to the latest methods developed in some of the German principalities, which Dr. Franklin said were the most advanced in the world.

Above all, a free education would be offered to every boy and girl in the country. The children of the poor artisan, the frontier homestead maker, and the able-bodied seaman would be offered the same opportunities as the children of the wealthy planter, the prosperous merchant, and the well-to-do shipowner.

This concept may have been the single most important principle developed in the United States during the period of the Confederation. No one knew precisely where it had originated. Benjamin Franklin was given the credit, but he denied that the thought had been his. He had advocated universal free education and had publicized the idea, he said, but the spark had not been his. Instead, he declared, it had sprung into being out of the aspirations of the people themselves. Was he being modest, or was he telling the truth? No one has ever known.

Whether the credit belongs to Franklin or someone else does not matter, however. What is important is that the entire nation eagerly adopted the idea. Here, in a nutshell, was the extension of the Age of Reason to its ultimate end. Here was the flowering of the Enlightenment as it was not known to people in any other land.

At first glance it may seem strange that the concept of universal free education should have had its origins in a raw land inhabited by the "dregs" of Europe—indentured servants, convicts, bankrupts, illiterate peasants. But a closer examination of these people indicates that they, far more than those who remained behind in the Old World, should have sought such a goal.

To them the New World represented more than escape from grinding poverty, miserable living conditions, and oppression of all kinds—political, personal, and religious. America meant opportunity. From the time of the first Jamestown settlement in 1607, America had meant equality. Every man was as good as his neighbor. Every man had the same chance to make good as every other man. Every man, by working hard and depending upon himself, could improve his lot and rise higher in the world than his father ever could.

It was small wonder that the principle had not developed in Great Britain and Europe, where rigid class lines existed, where the gulf between the rich and poor could not be bridged. In England the children of aristocrats enjoyed every luxury and were trained from birth for leadership. The children of the poor attended no schools and went to work in factories, often at the age of five or six. In France, Spain, and many other countries, the wealth was concentrated in the hands of the nobility and clergy; many of the former were decadent, and many of the latter were corrupt.

But the spirit of America was different. A brawny dock cargo handler, illiterate and poor, thought of himself as being the equal of his employer, John Hancock, a millionaire and distinguished statesman. What was more, Hancock thought of the longshoreman as his equal. They addressed one another by their first names. It is true that the cargo handler did not dine at the Hancock mansion on Beacon Hill in Boston, where he would have been embarrassed by living conditions so unlike his own. But he would have been horrified—and so would Hancock—by the mere suggestion that he tip his cap or tug his forelock when greeting his employer.

During the period of the Confederation new schools multiplied everywhere in the United States at such a rapid rate that it is impossible to obtain accurate statistics on the growth. It is known, however, that elementary schools expanded by at least four to one, and possibly five to one. Scores of academies for boys were opened in every state and frontier community, and at least forty academies for girls came into being. Existing colleges more than quadrupled their enrollment, at least eleven new colleges were established, and more than thirty others were planned.

Americans were proud of their intellectual achievements, and Benjamin Franklin, who was acclaimed in Europe as well as at home, was their greatest source of pride. Two painters, Benjamin West and John Singleton Copley, had achieved international reputations. English-born Thomas Paine was considered a philosopher and author of note, as was Sam Adams, the "father of the Revolution," whose propaganda thrusts at England had played such a large part in preparing Americans for their fight for independence.

John Singleton Copley of Boston was the single most important figure in the world of art, and even those people who had never set eyes on his paintings bragged about him. His work was exhibited in Paris and Berlin, Milan and Rome. Now that the war had ended, his paintings were being shown in London, too. "He is a genius," said the Boston *Advertiser* happily, "like no other in our land. We, who a few years ago were a race of savages, have nurtured a master of the brush."

Philadelphia was equally proud of Benjamin West, and the Pennsylvania *Gazette* called him "one of the foremost historical painters of the age." It is interesting that posterity has confirmed this judgment.

The painter John Trumbull, who served in the Continental Army as an aide to Washington, has been called the pictorial chronicler of the American Revolution. He later studied under Benjamin West in London, and spent several years in Europe. After his return to the United States, he was commissioned to decorate the rotunda of the Capitol in Washington with four large panels representing significant events of his country's struggle for independence.

Everywhere budding architects and landscape gardeners were experimenting with new styles. In music, the nation was gaining a sense of appreciation hitherto lacking, and concerts were given in all the major cities and towns. A few sculptors made an appearance, too, but the climate was not ripe for them, and they vanished again into the mists of obscurity.

Above all, perhaps, America saw herself as a refuge for the downhearted and oppressed of Europe. That feeling was best expressed, perhaps, by a poem that appeared in the Massachusetts *Centinel* on March 27, 1784:

Where happy millions
Their own fields possess,
No tyrant awes them,
And no lords oppress.

Immigrants began to arrive in ever increasing numbers as soon as the fighting stopped. It is not strange that most came from Great Britain, where the working classes long had felt a sympathy for and kinship with Americans. The majority were Scotsmen and Irishmen, with a smattering from the mill towns of the English Midlands. These people were heartily sick of working in the new factories that were springing up everywhere in the British Isles—men and women who loathed the abominable working conditions they were forced to endure and who, quite naturally, sought something better in life for themselves and their children.

They arrived in the major port cities, Boston, Philadelphia, New York, Baltimore, and Charleston, where housing facilities were inadequate. Postwar food prices were high, as has already been seen, and jobs in the cities were scarce because of the economic problems that were handicapping the United States.

Most of the new arrivals were "land hungry," as the Pennsylvania *Gazette* commented, but even those who might have preferred to remain in the towns were forced by circumstances to go out to the frontier, where land was either available at no cost or in return for a nominal sum.

Most of the newcomers poured out across the mountains to Kentucky and Franklin (Tennessee). Thousands of others went to the fertile Ohio Valley, and smaller numbers settled in the western portions of Georgia and South Carolina.

Perhaps the most astonishing feature of the immigration was the ability of these new arrivals to adapt themselves to the wilderness. They soon acquired the thinking and emotional patterns of Americans who had lived in the

New World all their lives. The United States was already the melting pot that it came to be called in the late nineteenth century, after the Civil War, when immigrants by the millions came to the country they considered the Promised Land.

Necessity was a grim teacher. Men who had never held axes in their hands chopped down trees. Men who had never built anything for themselves made log cabins for their families. Men unfamiliar with spades dug up tree roots to prepare their fields. Men who had never grown crops became farmers.

Children accustomed to the cities and towns of the British Isles made themselves at home in the wilderness, and thought nothing of walking five or ten miles to and from their one-room schoolhouses each day. Women who all their lives had bought food and clothing in shops now spun their own cloth, separated chaff from grain to obtain wheat, and pounded corn to make meal.

But it was the attitude of the newcomers that most reflected their rapid adaptation to the American way. They, who had known hardship and oppression, became fiercely independent. Having been given the opportunity to raise their heads high, they developed an intense pride, not only in themselves, but in their neighborhoods, their villages, and their states.

No naturalization requirements stood in the way of speedy assimilation. As soon as a newcomer arrived, had acquired land, and built himself a cabin, he was a citizen. He was expected to make himself available for militia duty and take part in the incessant frontier warfare with the Indians who, having been dispossessed, fought to regain the land they considered their own. The new citizen had the right to vote, and, no matter how new he was to the land, his voice was as loud as that of his neighbor.

Circumstances made the period of the Confederation an oddity in regard to immigration. Although society along the Eastern seaboard had become cultured, sophisticated, and complex, most of the new arrivals moved far inland. As a consequence, they lived and worked under conditions similar to those of the seaboard itself a half century to a century earlier. This strange quirk of circumstance, more than any other factor, accounts for the ease of the Confederation immigrants' assimilation. They became Americans literally overnight because they were forced into the same mold that had fashioned previous generations of Americans.

No one in a position of power and influence in the United States appears to have recognized the impact that the Industrial Revolution would have on the young nation. Machines that made products of every type and nature were already transforming England and the German principalities. The beginnings of mass manufacture were a factor in the great political upheavals that shook France in 1789. The Industrial Revolution shook Holland, and soon would spread to many other European nations.

But America seemed to remain untouched. Her few factories were tiny, family-owned places where goods were still made by hand. Machines and assembly lines were virtually unknown. No one living in that era would have believed that, in little more than a century, the United States would become the greatest power on earth, thanks largely to her vast and efficient industrial production.

Americans were close to the earth that provided them with the essentials of life. The few large cities were not popular, and the majority of their inhabitants did not live there by choice. Every man's ideal was that of owning his own home, far from his nearest neighbors.

The most respected Americans had already achieved that goal. General Washington lived on a large plantation in Virginia. John Adams owned a farm at Braintree, Massachusetts. Thomas Jefferson and Patrick Henry owned rural retreats. Even the famous physician Dr. Benjamin Rush and others like him spent as little time as possible in their town houses, and went to their country homes whenever possible.

It was Jefferson who was the spokesman for the joys of an agrarian society. Repeatedly in his writing he spoke of the discomforts and evils of city dwelling, the satisfactions and accomplishments of country living. He was convinced the United States would become a powerful agrarian nation, and it did not occur to him that she would be touched by the Industrial Revolution.

Alexander Hamilton was one of a very few who dimly felt the pressures of what actually lay ahead for the United States. To an extent, his belief that the Confederation was too weak to handle the problems of a complex urban society was based upon his vague realization that the nation would become increasingly industrial, rather than rural.

It must be stressed that the collapse of the Confederation was not in any way caused by the process of industrialization. That did not come until much later. The United States was mainly a nation of farmers, and the overwhelming majority gloried in their lot and pitied the unfortunates who were forced to live in cities and the urban dwellers of Britain and Europe, and would not willingly change places with anyone.

Americans sensed the growing importance of their new, weak nation, and believed that their Revolution was of long-lasting significance as a major force in world history. Perhaps because their own background was so bare they were fascinated by history.

The Reverend Jeremy Belknap, a Harvard graduate who was minister of a Congregational church at Dover, New Hampshire, was such a man. Soon after the Revolution he was transferred to the Federal Street Church in Boston, where he remained until the close of the century. He was a founder of the Massachusetts Historical Society, and wrote a three-volume history of New Hampshire that was a standard reference work for more than one hundred and fifty years. It is still used by scholars today.

Other clergymen wrote comprehensive, remarkably objective histories of the Revolution itself. One was Dr. David Ramsay of Charleston, South Carolina, who was also a prominent figure in the political life of that state. Born in Pennsylvania, he was graduated from the College of New Jersey, later Princeton. In addition to his divinity degree, he obtained an M.D. from the College of Pennsylvania, and practiced medicine in South Carolina. His father-in-law was Henry Laurens, one of the South's most distinguished statesmen.

Dr. Ramsay did more than write history; he helped to make it. He served in the South Carolina legislature, was a member of the Continental Congress for three years, and subsequently spent another six years as president of the South Carolina senate.

His first book told the story of the Revolution in South Carolina, and was a clear, dispassionate work, except that he attacked two British generals with great vigor. Lord Cornwallis and Lord Rawdon had both fought against the patriots in South Carolina, and Ramsay assaulted them with blunt, partisan vigor. He was so forthright, in fact, that even years later no publisher in England would print the book.

Dr. Ramsay's second book, published in 1789, was a general history of the Revolution. He wrote with spirit, but the work was marred by typographical errors and occasional mistakes in fact. It became very popular, however, and influenced the thinking of several generations of Americans.

The Reverend William Gordon was an even more remarkable man. An English clergyman, he came to Massachusetts in 1770, and became pastor of a Congregational church at Roxbury. He was soon active in the Revolutionary movement, and also became an overseer of Harvard College.

Early in the Revolution, perhaps only a month or two after it began in the spring of 1775, he conceived the idea of writing a complete history of the war. His interest in this project grew until, in 1778, he resigned as pastor of his church in order to devote his full time to the book.

Virtually every important civilian and military official of high rank came to know William Gordon. John Hancock, in fact, once remarked jokingly that when an event of importance took place, Gordon was there to see it; if he wasn't present, Hancock observed, the event was meaningless.

In 1784 the clergyman, after repeated efforts, finally obtained permission from the Congress to study all its war records. He also prevailed upon General Washington to let him study the military records, as well as the correspondence and diary of the commander in chief.

After spending several months in Philadelphia, searching the files of Congress, William Gordon went to Washington's plantation at Mount Vernon, Virginia. There he remained for the better part of the summer. He began work at sunrise each day, and remained at Washington's desk until long after dark every evening. When he failed to understand something he read, or wanted a fuller explanation, he went to Washington for amplification. Often he ate breakfast or dinner with the General.

By the time historian Gordon returned to Massachusetts late in 1784, he had amassed huge quantities of material. He then spent the next two years writing a massive volume, which he called *The History of the Rise, Progress and Establishment of the Independence of the United States of America.*

Then his troubles began. It was the custom in the eighteenth century for an author to pay for the printing of a book himself, and get back the money through selling it in bookstores. But William Gordon had no money for this or any other purpose. In fact, he was living on the charity of friends who believed in him and his enterprise.

He had also made an enemy of the wealthiest, most influential man in Massachusetts, John Hancock. Unfortunately, Gordon had portrayed Hancock as vain and pompous, and even though this analysis was accurate, Hancock swore he would drive out of business any printer who agreed to work for the clergyman.

Gordon eventually decided to publish the book in England by selling subscriptions in advance. He went to London, and there encountered still more difficulties. The printers refused to touch his book because, they insisted, he was too biased in favor of the American cause. Eventually he did find a printer, however, and the book was published in 1787.

The History created an international sensation. It was praised in England as first-rate historical reporting, and proud Americans hailed it without reservation as a triumph. It became the biggest-selling book in the United States, and attracted a large audience in Great Britain, where it was purchased not only by scholars but by thousands who sympathized with the American cause.

William Gordon returned to Massachusetts a wealthy, famous man. His book was regarded as the authoritative history of the Revolution for more than a hundred years, and some of its findings are still useful to scholars in modern times. Only John Hancock refused to read it, or to recognize Gordon when they chanced to meet at the Bunch o' Grapes and other Boston inns.

No individual or group praised Gordon more lavishly than the talented Connecticut authors who called themselves the Hartford Wits. These men, among them John Trumbull, Joel Barlow, Dr. Lemuel Hopkins, David Humphreys, and Timothy Dwight, formed the nucleus of the first literary association in the United States. With the exception of Massachusetts-born Timothy Dwight, all were natives of Connecticut; all lived and worked there, and all were ardent patriots.

Trumbull, a teacher at Yale College who subsequently studied in the law office of John Adams and then became an attorney, was already famous because of *M'Fingal*. The work did not deserve the reputation it achieved, and was actually rather crude poetry. But Trumbull attacked the Tories with such vitriolic satire that he became renowned. It is interesting that in later years he lost faith in democracy, and by the time he died in 1831, in Detroit, he had become a Tory himself.

Timothy Dwight was one of the truly great men of his age. A clergyman who served as a military chaplain in the war, he wrote the song "Columbia," which was the most popular of its day and, for a generation, served as the unofficial national anthem of the United States. He also wrote a poem, "The Conquest of Canaan," which did not deserve the stir it created.

The real reputation of Dwight rests on his achievements as an educator and administrator. He became the president of Yale, where he introduced new methods of education that replaced antiquated systems used universally in the United States and Great Britain. He was also a firm believer in scientific research, and was a pioneer in hiring scientists of standing, obtaining funds they could use for purposes of research, and battling to preserve their academic freedom.

David Humphreys was a man with a badly inflated reputation, which was considerable in his own day. He was the author of several very bad poems, which were little better than doggerel. In them, however, he extolled the future greatness of America. This was what his fellow countrymen wanted to hear, and their enthusiasm for his vision made him famous. Romance saved him from the writing of more poetry, fortunately. He met an English girl who was a member of a wealthy family, and with the assistance of his father-in-law opened a plant in Hartford that made cloth. Eventually it became the most prosperous mill in the United States, and Humphreys was so busy that he inflicted no more of his writing on the public.

Joel Barlow was by far the best writer in the Hartford group, as well as the most talented in many fields. His epic poem, *The Vision of Columbus,* published in 1787, had genuine merit. It did not, however, deserve the praise heaped on it by Barlow's close friend, Noah Webster, the lexicographer, who called it "an inspired work of pure genius."

Barlow enjoyed many careers, all of them successful. A military chaplain in the Revolution, he became a lawyer, a politician, a land salesman for the Ohio Company in France, and, finally, a diplomat. He served as United States consul general at Algiers from 1795 to 1805, and was instrumental in winning treaties favorable to his country in the Barbary wars with the North African pirate states. He rose to the rank of minister, and his last post, in 1811–12, was that of Minister to France. A moody, mercurial man, Barlow had great literary talent, and posterity, like his contemporaries, has regretted the small size of his written output.

Another writer from Connecticut, and an educator who had a great impact in his own time as well as on future generations, was the Reverend Jedidiah Morse. A Yale graduate who became a Congregational clergyman, he was a religious and political conservative who developed an abiding passion for geography. His first book, *Geography Made Easy*, went through more than one hundred printings, twenty-six of them in his own lifetime. A later, more ambitious work, *The American Geography*, was considered a masterpiece, and also went through many editions. It won Morse international fame, an honorary degree from Edinburgh University, and a large fortune.

Noah Webster, a Hartford attorney already mentioned, had a greater influence on his own times and later ages than any other man who dealt with words. He wrote a large number of books, on many subjects, but his renown rests almost exclusively on his work as a lexicographer.

Webster published his first dictionary in 1806, and his great masterpiece was *An American Dictionary of the English Language*. The first of its almost countless editions appeared in 1828, and the name of Webster has been synonymous with that of dictionaries in the United States since his time.

"I first thought of preparing a dictionary during the days of the Confederation," Webster wrote. "We are a new people as well as a new nation, and when I realized we were speaking a new language unlike the English spoken—and written—in Great Britain, the need for an American dictionary became clear to me."

The key to America's cultural and artistic development, not to mention her unique political development, which culminated in the formulation of the Constitution, lay in Webster's phrase, "We are a new people."

Isolated from Europe by the Atlantic Ocean, surrounded on the north and west by sparsely settled wilderness, the United States indeed stood alone. Her people were subjected to their own forces and pressures rather than outside influences. Not the least of these was her remarkable rate of growth.

No one knows precisely how many immigrants came to the New World from Great Britain and the European continent during the years of the Confederation, but the influx probably took place at a rate of about one hundred thousand persons per year. This growth taxed the facilities of the new nation to the utmost. In fact, only because there was so much fertile land was the country able to absorb the newcomers.

Every American knew that land was the nation's greatest asset. There *was* so much of it! In all, within the boundaries of the United States as defined by the Treaty of 1783, lay more than a million square miles. Of this, approximately 250,000,000 acres was public-domain land, that is, land belonging to the Confederation or the state governments.

At least 40 percent of the total land, or 400,000 million square miles, was uninhabited except for roaming tribes of Indians. And everywhere else, even along the relatively heavily populated Atlantic seaboard, vast quantities of land could be purchased. It is no wonder that Americans remained buoyant and optimistic in spite of the nation's financial problems.

Yet America's greatest strength was, at the same time, one of her most debilitating weaknesses. She was so sparsely settled that major nations could abuse her with impunity. Although exact figures do not exist, some historians estimate that, at the beginning of the Revolution, there were about 2,750,000 people in the country. Of these, 600,000–700,000 were Negro slaves, most of them living in the states of the South.

The population crept higher very slowly during the war years. Then came the explosion. Soldiers were demobilized at the end of the war, married men went home to their families, and the bachelors took brides. Newspapers, periodicals, and the correspondence of the better educated indicates there was a baby boom during the era of the Confederation. This, combined with increased immigration, gave the nation approximately one million more persons during a period of about seven years.

As has already been seen, most of the new arrivals traveled to the West. They were joined by the unhappy, the restless, and the unemployed of the seaboard. Patrick Henry, himself settling on the frontier with his family when he retired from politics, took note of this extraordinary phenomenon when he wrote, "We are a people on the move, a people seeking perfection in our lives, for ourselves and our children, just as we seek fertile land and freedom."

James Monroe, a young Virginia surveyor who would become the fifth President of the United States, saw this mass migration through the eyes of youth. "We march," he wrote, "by the thousands and tens of thousands into the forests of pine and oak, into the land of swift-rushing rivers and sweet-scented earth. Although we are few in number, our future is plain for all to read. We are destined for greatness, we are destined to become an immortal breed."

There were few in the nation who would have denied the validity of a claim that Europeans, had they known of it, would have called absurd and extravagant. Americans felt themselves destined to be strong and great. Their problems were grave, their finances shaky, their form of government unwieldy and weak.

But their self-confidence was as boundless as the one million square miles they occupied, as the millions of additional square miles into which, they felt certain, they would some day expand. It was this conviction, above all else, that made them an "immortal breed."

V. Expansion and Improvements

In 1769 an energetic and fearless young land surveyor, hunter, and trapper first crossed the mountains and wandered into the heavily wooded bluegrass country that came to be known as Kentucky. Daniel Boone returned to Virginia, which claimed the region, and extolled its virtues before going west again to settle. A handful of others, most of them adventure seekers, followed him during the next six years. At the outbreak of the Revolution in 1775, the population of Kentucky is estimated to have been between one and two hundred Americans, all of them men. The area was too wild, the Indian tribes were too dangerous for women to settle in the wilderness.

During the war years, the population of Kentucky increased very slowly. By 1783, a generous estimate might place her total population at five hundred persons, including a few women. Then came the great population explosion.

According to the census of 1790, which was admittedly incomplete, the population of the Kentucky district of

Virginia numbered 73,677 people. A scant two years later, when Kentucky achieved statehood, its population had jumped by approximately 20,000 more. The Franklin district of North Carolina was somewhat better known in the pre-Revolutionary period, and in 1775 the area had a population of about 7,000. It had jumped to 35,000 when the census of 1790 was taken, and then, suddenly booming, that number was tripled in the next few years. When Tennessee became a state in 1796, it had a total population of more than 100,000.

The frontier expanded in directions other than westward across the Alleghenies. In 1775, according to scornful citizens of New Hampshire, the population of Vermont consisted of "a handful of ruffians who call themselves Green Mountain Boys, a few cattle and many green trees." In 1784, Vermont, which had proclaimed itself an independent state in 1777, had grown to 30,000 men, women, and children. In 1791, when it became the fourteenth state, Vermont had almost 100,000, and had more than tripled her population in seven years.

The cities of the seaboard increased, too, even though only a relatively small number of immigrants decided they preferred metropolitan living to farm life on the frontier. By the time the era of the Confederation came to an end in 1789, Philadelphia, America's first city, had a total population of more than 40,000. New York had grown to 30,000, passing Boston, and had become the second city of the nation.

But the true indication of the American metropolitan growth during this period was in wealth rather than mere size. In spite of the nation's economic and financial difficulties, the coming of peace enabled men to prosper as never before. In the summer of 1785 alone, for example, more than six hundred residents of Philadelphia built handsome new red brick houses for their families. And Baltimore, a city with a newly acquired dignity in 1786, had grown in three years from 6,000 persons to more than 15,000. Aware that their town had become a real city, its citizens decided to look and act the part. Accordingly, they taxed themselves for cobblestones to pave eighty square blocks of roads.

Obtaining the cobblestones proved almost impossible. Small factories in Philadelphia and New York made paving blocks, but none were equipped to turn out enough for such a gigantic order. So the people of Baltimore banded together and built their own plant for the purpose. Thereafter, it provided cobblestones for most of the cities and towns on the Atlantic seaboard, and American pride became so great that even small towns preferred heavy taxes and paving blocks to raw dirt roads!

The problems of the bustling cities sound familiar to the modern reader who is aware of urban difficulties of the present day. People in Philadelphia, New York, and Boston complained bitterly that there weren't enough physicians on hand to protect the health of the people. According to the Massachusetts *Centinel:* "Were an epidemic to break out, thousands would die. Boston has not the doctors to heal a multitude of the sickly, nor enough beds in her hospitals to nurse them back to health."

Another complaint was expressed frequently. "The

masons of Philadelphia," said the Pennsylvania *Gazette* in 1787, "soon will be earning incomes greater than that of our distinguished Dr. Franklin!"

The newspaper was exaggerating, but it was true that skilled artisans commanded exorbitantly high wages. New York carpenters earned more than attorneys at law; Baltimore stonemasons made more money than the captains of merchant ships. And rents in every major city were so high that landlords, city dwellers throughout the country agreed, made more than anyone.

It is fascinating to see how history repeats itself. In present times, New Haven, Connecticut, has been a pioneer in urban redevelopment. Slum dwellings have been torn down and replaced by comfortable, low-cost housing projects. New office buildings, department stores and shops, parks and playgrounds, and schools have made the city a more attractive commerical center. In short, New Haven has set an example for scores of other cities throughout the United States.

New Haven performed precisely the same function during the period of the Confederation. In 1783, she formed a new kind of city government to handle the problems of a growing community. Her people formed a corporation, to be headed by a mayor, a board of aldermen, and a city council. No other community in North America had ever known such officials previously.

All were to be elected by the citizens. And every male New Haven dweller who was twenty-one years of age or over was granted automatic citizenship. It was even proposed that voting be made compulsory, but the notion

This is an

EXAMINATION COPY

From

THOMAS NELSON INC.

250 Park Avenue, New York, N. Y. 10017

Please accept this book with our compliments. We would appreciate receiving a copy of any evaluation or listing which may result from your examination. Comments about our books from teachers and librarians are of great interest and much appreciated.

proved too radical, and the citizens, voting on the idea, rejected it as a form of "tyranny."

The principal function of the corporation was that of making the city an efficiently managed community. Its goals were the achievement of a "healthy center of commerce, literature and education." Specifically, the corporation was directed to improve the harbor and extend the wharves, to encourage the building of new warehouses, to cut canals, and to pave all city streets and improve their appearance by planting each with double rows of elms. Other charges were the building of adequate schools, hospitals, and almshouses.

The corporation went to work with vigor. Full cooperation was offered to Yale College whenever it needed the city's help. Only one provision was attached: Yale students were sometimes unruly, and the city said it would not cooperate with the school if there were frequent public brawls involving the student body.

Energetic steps were taken by the corporation to form what it called literary establishments. Men of letters were offered special tax incentives and good houses if they would move to the city, and several inns and taverns, encouraged by the aldermen and council, announced plans to cater to a "literary trade." It was the hope of New Haven that it could become the rival of Hartford as the center of America's intellectual life.

"The enlightened patriotism of a few," said the Pennsylvania *Gazette* on February 18, 1784, commenting on the developments in New Haven, "will cause the prosperity of this new city; may it become rich and flourishing, as it is already the most salubrious and elegant on the continent."

Improvements were made in many other fields. Patriotic citizens with strong humanitarian feelings recognized the need for more hospitals and poorhouses in every major community. Realizing that only a few people had enough money to do something concrete, they banded together in associations and groups to provide funds for the building and maintenance of such institutions.

When these means proved effective, they also formed groups, societies, and associations for a variety of other purposes. Enthusiastic Americans joined in private organizations to build roads and bridges, to dig canals, to found institutions of higher learning, and to build and maintain orphan asylums.

One sign of the ferment of the times was the sudden appearance of new newspapers and magazines. Scores appeared in every part of the country during the era of the Confederation. It has been said that there were more newspapers per citizen in the United States at this time than in any other land.

The humanitarian movement also spread in other directions. Previously there had been only one art museum in the country, in Charleston. Now, between 1784 and 1788, eleven others were founded. Philadelphia, Boston, and New York had grown large enough and sophisticated enough to have developed an interest in the arts, and it is not surprising that museums were established in those cities. It is significant, however, that a frontier fort in the West, Pittsburgh, should have cared enough about culture at this early stage of growth to have built a three-room log cabin "with windows large enough to allow the bric-a-brac and objects of art to be seen by all," as a museum. Another, located in Erie, Pennsylvania, encouraged citizens of the town and surrounding countryside to submit works of art for exhibition.

Equally important was the beginning of the trend to improve the lot of all men. This extended to sharp reforms in penal conditions during the era of the Confederation. The thirteen American colonies had followed the example of England, and prison life was a nightmare for the inmates. Prisoners were beaten and subjected to cruel treatment, including torture. Their housing conditions were miserable, and when they weren't being starved, they considered themselves fortunate to eat the bad food they were given for their meals.

This situation did not fit in with the American concept of a better, more humane world for all mankind. Criminal codes were revised and made less harsh, less demanding. Debtors' prisons were not abolished until the following century, however, so a man still could be locked away for years, given no chance to earn the money to pay off his creditors.

The separation of state and church is a basic tenet of American philosophy and government, with freedom of worship guaranteed in the Constitution. This separation took place during the period of the Confederation. Previously, of course, the majority of the colonies had an "official" church, the Anglican Church, with the King of England as its titular head. There were notable exceptions, of course. In New England, little Rhode Island was a fortress of religious freedom for all. The colony had been an outgrowth of Providence Plantations, founded by the Reverend Roger Williams, who had left Massachusetts Bay because he had not been able to tolerate the Puritans' insistence that everyone accept their form of worship.

Throughout most of New England, the Congregational Church dominated in size, prestige, and influence, although it never had been the official church. Pennsylvania had been founded by William Penn, whose charter had specifically granted him the right to establish his Society of Friends there. The Quakers, as the Friends were known, took great pains to grant total freedom of religion to all creeds. And the charter of Maryland specifically granted Roman Catholics the right to worship there.

Some of the most influential men in the new United States belonged to no church organization. Indeed, they were insistent that there be no official church from the time the Declaration of Independence was signed. Most of this group can be identified as deists, that is, they believed in God but did not accept any particular religion. The Unitarian Church subsequently grew out of their attitudes.

Among the leaders of this group were Thomas Jefferson, the enormously influential Benjamin Franklin, John Adams, and Thomas Paine. Patrick Henry was nominally an Anglican, but he, perhaps more than anyone else, demanded the separation of church and state.

The constitutions of the individual states guaranteed freedom of religion for all. As John Adams said, "When we can enlarge our minds to allow each other an entire liberty in religious matters, the human race will be more happy and more respectable in this and the future stage of its existence."

In spite of the growing trend toward freedom, certain inequalities persisted. New Jersey allowed only Protestants to hold public office. Delaware insisted that all of its officials believe in the Trinity, which excluded liberal Protestants, deists, and Jews.

It is interesting to note that no guarantees of religious freedom were included in the original version of the Constitution, although state and church were separated. Such men as Patrick Henry and Thomas Jefferson campaigned so successfully for tolerance, however, that the guarantee all Americans enjoy was the rallying point for the so-called Bill of Rights, the first ten amendments to the Constitution, which included the guarantee of religious freedom.

The movement to abolish slavery also was organized on a large scale during the age of the Confederation. The movement actually began when an abolitionist society was formed in 1774, with Benjamin Franklin—naturally! —as its president. During the long war the organization was inactive, but George Bryan, a Pennsylvanian who was a friend of Franklin, was responsible for the passage of a state law, in 1780, ordering the abolition of slavery in Pennsylvania.

The abolitionist society was reorganized in 1784. It encouraged the formation of similar societies in other states, and enjoyed considerable success. In 1785 a society came into being in New York, with John Jay as president and Alexander Hamilton as secretary. New York enjoyed the distinction of being the first state to rid itself of its slaves. A law ordering gradual abolition was passed by the New York legislature in 1786; there were evasions, to be sure, but, for all practical purposes, slavery was ended in New York by the time the Constitution became the law of the land in 1789.

Abolition societies also sprang up in a number of other states during the Confederation years. One in little Delaware was particularly active, and the movement spread to its neighbors, New Jersey and Maryland. Connecticut societies took the lead in New England, and were followed by sister groups in Rhode Island. Oddly, the movement was slow in forming and even slower in its growth in Massachusetts, which was thought of by its citizens as the cradle of liberty for all Americans.

Abolitionist activities were not confined to the North. Nowhere were the most distinguished citizens more active than in Virginia, where slaveholding was common. It is not surprising that Patrick Henry, who was devoted to freedom for all men in all things, should take the lead. He also set an example for his fellow Virginians by setting free his own slaves and then hiring them at decent wages as household servants and field workers.

"There are many reasons I will die a poor man," he wrote in 1787. "Chief amongst them is the sum I must spend each year in wages to my staff. Far better that I be poor so that they may be free!"

General Washington, although himself a slave owner, was convinced that the shameful institution should be abolished. A far-seeing man, he believed emancipation should be gradual in order to prevent the economy of the

South, which already depended upon slave labor, from suffering a crippling blow.

Liberty-loving Jefferson accepted Washington's approach and also fought for gradual abolition. James Madison, who would become the nation's fourth President, was more drastic. Emerging during the Confederation as a leader of national stature, and, during the latter part of the period the principal author of the Constitution, he was deeply impressed by Henry's gesture. So, in 1788, he did the same, making a great personal sacrifice, since he owned a large number of slaves.

Such gestures and activities had little effect in the South, where slaveholders fought successfully to strengthen state laws that made it difficult for people to free their slaves. But the influence of men like Washington, Jefferson, and Madison extended far beyond the boundaries of any one state, and their beliefs, combined with their activities, helped to persuade many in the North to join abolitionist societies. Henry, who always thought in terms of his beloved Virginia, confined his activities to his own state.

Perhaps the most unusual movement in the United States during the Confederation years was one that began in Boston and spread to Philadelphia. The Humane Society, as the organization called itself, was concerned with helping the victims of what it called suspended animation. A later age would say these victims were ill or injured.

The basic cause of suspended animation, according to officials on the Humane Society in both cities, was "near-drowning." A number of machines and devices were invented to prevent drowning. One was a cumbersome affair that squeezed water from the lungs of a person rescued from the water. It went out of favor because, more often than not, it also broke the victim's ribs. These devices were made available to any group living near water that requested them. The Boston Society also put up little rescue huts at various spots along the Massachusetts coast where shipwrecks occurred fairly frequently.

Sunstroke was another cause of suspended animation, as was being struck by lightning. The correspondence of the secretary of the Philadelphia Humane Society revealed sorrow, however, that not one of four victims of lightning could be revived. Other causes were the drinking of excess quantities of laudanum, a crude form of opium used as an anesthetic, and drinking large quantities of cold water when overheated.

Still another cause was listed as "near-hanged." Neither the Boston nor Philadelphia branch of the Society recorded any cases in this category, nor was any explanation given. The modern reader must be content to wonder what the eighteenth-century American humanists might have meant.

Charitable works were very important to the well-to-do citizen. Since most of the country's wealth came from foreign trade, it is not surprising that many organizations directed their efforts to relieve ill or injured sailors and the families of men lost at sea. Philadelphia, conscious of its prosperity, its size, and its standing as the nation's capital, led the way. A Society for the Relief of the Widows of Decayed Pilots was formed in 1783, before the peace treaty had been signed. Early the following year, another organization, Society for the Relief of Indigent Mariners, received the support of the city's prominent families. And in 1785, still another group made its appearance, the Society for the Relief of Poor and Distressed Masters of Ships, Their Widows and Children.

Philadelphia was concerned with other types of welfare, too. A Corporation for the Relief and Employment of the Poor enlisted the assistance of several hundred citizens, and eventually sponsored an orphan asylum. Eventually, a decade later, it also built a hospital for the "care of poor women, chiefly widows."

The Massachusetts Charitable Society was founded in 1780 for the purpose of helping poverty-stricken sailors and their families. In 1784, when the entire nation was becoming conscious of religious tolerance, this organization added a new clause to its charter. Persons of all faiths were eligible for assistance, and no one was to be denied help because of his religious beliefs. In addition to helping widows and orphans and the poor, the Massachusetts Charitable Society founded a school "for the education of the daughters of the poor."

New York was slower than the other large cities to form charitable societies. The principal reason is obvious: New York, after suffering under enemy occupation since the early days of the war, needed time to recover its own balance. The wealthy were forced to put their own houses in order before they could turn to the help of the poor.

When the city acted, however, it moved with a determination and energy that eventually made it the largest and most prosperous in the Western Hemisphere. In 1786, the Black Friars were organized. This group, which also met for social purposes, had as its goal the "alleviation of all distresses among the poor." Eight hundred of the most prominent New Yorkers joined. Alexander Hamilton was the first president, and John Jay was the first vice president. Two members of the prominent Schuyler family of Albany were members of the original board of trustees. This organization collected so much money that, within five years, it acquired a working capital of more than $200,000. This was the equivalent of over $3,000,000 today. This fund continued to grow rapidly, and in 1800 the Black Friars became so wealthy that three new organizations were formed within the parent group. The treasury was split, and the new societies branched out to do charitable work of all kinds.

Richmond, Virginia, was one of America's new towns, and during the Confederation put up its first buildings of brick and stone. Its residents were very conscious of their obligation to the poor, and in 1784, a society was formed for the relief of "strangers in difficulties and distress who require financial assistance and the moral support of the more fortunate."

By 1788, there were two active charitable clubs in Baltimore, with two more in the process of organization. Two were busy in Wilmington, two in Trenton, and three in Hartford. In civic-minded New Haven, there were five.

Charleston was unique. Of all major American cities, it alone did not wait until after the Revolution to become busy in helping the poor. In 1769, the Fellowship Society was founded there, and was something of a model for similar organizations elsewhere. It sought contributions from all citizens able to pay and remained active through the entire war, including the years of British occupation. Half of the funds it raised went for the education of children who would not have been able to afford schooling without help. The other half was expended on the insane, the first instance of assistance in the nation for those suffering from mental and emotional problems. Charlestonians referred to these persons as "deplorable maniacs."

The first temperance societies in the country were formed during the Confederation era, too. The ever active Dr. Benjamin Rush of Philadelphia founded one in 1782, but it languished. He did not give up, however, and when he tried again in 1788, several hundred Philadelphians gave time and money to halt the abuses of overindulgence in alcoholic beverages. In spite of Rush's optimism, the movement did not spread and, except for several branches in Connecticut, did not gain general popular acceptance.

Immigration became so heavy once peace was ensured that every seaboard city was forced to found immigrant-aid societies. There were Irish and Scottish societies in every major town and metropolitan center. Within a short time, these clubs became useful tools in the hands of politicians, who ladled out help in small quantities in return for the votes of the newcomers. A disgusted Thomas Jefferson condemned most of these organizations, saying their activities "subvert the principles upon which a truly democratic society is based."

The exceptions were the clubs founded from Boston to Baltimore by Americans of German extraction. These societies had no goal other than the aid of German immigrants, and were exceptionally efficient. Beginning in 1784, all Germans who came to the United States were requested to register at a local headquarters established in every port city. There the newcomer was questioned at length regarding his financial situation and vocation, and help was given him accordingly.

Those who needed jobs were provided with work. Those whose families were ill received free medical treatment. Free legal assistance was available for those who might require the services of an attorney. In fact, the German aid societies were so thorough that its members visited ships arriving in the ports to make certain the immigrants had not been mistreated. When abuses were found, appropriate legal action was taken to ensure that they were not repeated.

After the German immigrant settled into a job and a dwelling, often a house provided by the society, the members continued to guide him. German-American ladies called on the immigrant women to cheer them and make them feel at home. German children were educated in special schools established to teach them English quickly and painlessly. Scholarships were provided for young immigrant German youths of merit, too. The Philadelphia society alone provided scholarships for eighteen such young men from the inception of the program in 1784 until the adoption of the Constitution in 1789.

Libraries were to be found everywhere in the United States. The first of them was established in Philadelphia, in 1731, by Benjamin Franklin. Every self-respecting town with a population of no more than three or four thousand had its own library at the outbreak of the Revolution.

These organizations became inactive during the war years, but virtually all reopened soon after. The one notable exception was the Newport Library, which had been burned by the British during their occupation of the Rhode Island seaport. Although few Americans believed it, the British always claimed that the burning had been accidental.

The history of *privately* endowed libraries during the era of the Confederation runs counter of that of other humanitarian and cultural developments. Many libraries were forced to close their doors, particularly in New England and the Mid-Atlantic states. This seems odd, particularly in view of the growth in other aesthetic spheres. But the puzzle is easily understood: Library societies were, in the main, snobbish social organizations. They were not founded to provide the public with reading material, but served as gathering places for gentlemen of wealth, who liked to meet in book-lined clubrooms. Apparently they had no place in an America passionately devoted to the principles and practice of democracy.

One of the most noted of the associations formed in the 1780's was the distinguished American Academy of Arts and Sciences, which is still in existence. It was founded at the beginning of the decade under a charter granted by the Massachusetts legislature, and owed its existence largely to the zeal of John Adams. The nation's principal representative in Europe for several years, he discovered that the most admired of New World organizations was Franklin's American Philosophical Society, which had been founded before the war and was subjected to a sweeping reorganization in 1780. Wanting to increase his country's prestige still more, Adams worked for the organization of the American Academy.

Its success was immediate, and in 1785 it issued the first of its respected papers, a volume called *Memoirs,* a book containing articles on economic, scientific, and literary subjects. Members of the Academy were men of self-confidence willing to debate issues, in print, with Franklin's awe-inspiring Philosophical Society.

The latter organization resumed its activities at the same high level at which it had operated prior to the war. In 1785, when Franklin returned from his mission as special Minister to France, he immediately took charge of the project again, and a few months later it, too, published a volume. This consisted chiefly of an account of the members' debates during the preceding years, and was eagerly read and praised by American intellectuals. It was also greeted enthusiastically in Europe, where any activity by Benjamin Franklin was sure to be received by an admiring and sympathetic audience.

The success of the Philosophical Society and the American Academy prompted imitations elsewhere. A society was founded in New York, a second in New Haven, and a third in Hartford. But the genius of Franklin and the organizational ability of Adams were lacking. Perhaps the climate was not yet ripe. For whatever the reasons, attendance at meetings was poor, subscriptions were few, and all three organizations died away within a year or two, lamented by no one.

The American Medical Society had been formed in Philadelphia prior to the war, but did not flourish until the years of the Confederation. Meanwhile, in 1781, the physicians of Boston banded together to form the Massachusetts Medical Society. The aim of this group was the same as that of the American Medical Society. The doctors wanted to establish codes of ethical practice, insist on standards for admission to the profession, and keep watch over all physicians to make certain there were no abuses. The Society also established standard fees in order to prevent the unscrupulous from charging their patients too much.

In 1782, Harvard formed its Medical School, hiring an administrator and three physicians for its faculty. There was an immediate conflict between the School and the Society, each claiming the right to promote medical research and to regard itself as the final authority in the establishment of codes. Neither group was hurt by the conflict, which resulted in swift research development, soaring standards, and increased prestige for everyone concerned. In an age when barbers and innumerable quacks practiced medicine—to the harm of their patients —the general public enjoyed the greatest benefit from the dispute.

The first medical school in the country had been opened by the University of Pennsylvania in 1765. The establishment of a medical school by Harvard reduced the dependence of American students on Edinburgh School of Medicine, in Scotland, where more than sixty young men from the United States were studying in the years immediately following the war. America was coming of age in education, and there was an academic ferment everywhere.

King's College, in New York, which had been closed

during the war, reopened its doors as Columbia College, and, in a bold and vigorous recruiting campaign, offered higher wages to professors than any other school in the country.

Yale expanded rapidly, doubling its faculty in the years immediately following the war. Plans to set up a rival school in Hartford were abandoned, and the Hartford civic leaders, in a display of common sense rare in any age, gave Yale their unqualified support.

The College of New Jersey, soon to become Princeton, repaired its war-damaged buildings, added others to its campus, and hired a number of teachers. Included were several foreign classicists recommended by James Madison, an alumnus. Meanwhile, the legislature of Pennsylvania made an impressive land grant to a new school, Dickinson College, and the state became the first to support more than one major institution of higher learning.

Georgia, the newest and poorest of the states, also passed a bill through its legislature providing land and funds for a state college. This stung North and South Carolina into action, and both quickly followed Georgia's example.

Perhaps the most dramatic improvements took place at the College of William and Mary, in Virginia. Thomas Jefferson, an alumnus of the Williamsburg school, wanted to see some university in the South rival Harvard as a seat of learning, and naturally thought of his own alma mater. At his instigation, the College of William and Mary set up a law school. This was a new concept, as most attorneys approached their profession by entering the law offices of someone already in practice and spending a year or two as apprentices before taking a bar examination.

Jefferson, before leaving to become United States Minister to France in 1785, was responsible for another innovation at William and Mary. He sparked the hiring of professors of French; the following year the school also added to its faculty a teacher of German and another of Spanish. The idea of teaching modern languages was unique. Universities and colleges throughout the world taught the classics, Greek and Latin. But it had never before occurred to anyone to include modern languages in a college curriculum.

The demand for improved transportation facilities throughout the United States was as great as that for increased educational facilities. Everyone was convinced the nation would grow rapidly, but the rate of actual expansion was so swift it exceeded the expectations of even the most optimistic. There were demands for more ships and intercity public coach service, for roads and bridges and canals.

Urgent calls came from men in every walk of life for canals that would be used for purposes of internal trade, for the moving of raw materials from the interior to the seaboard. Leading the movement was General Washington, who as a young surveyor before the war had concocted with Thomas Johnson of Maryland a scheme to develop the headwaters of the Potomac River in Virginia, and, after broadening the river into a navigable channel, establishing a new city at its mouth. He revived that project now.

In 1785, the Virginia legislature granted a charter to the Potomac Company, and purchased 20 percent of its stock. A few months later, Maryland followed suit, granting an almost identical charter and purchasing 15 percent of the organization's stock. The project turned out to be far more difficult than anyone had anticipated, chiefly because the scientific problems of dredging and broadening a river had never before been faced by Americans. Work progressed slowly, but at no time did it stop, and by the end of the War of 1812, almost 350 miles of the Potomac had been opened to all shipping except the deepest-draft oceangoing vessels.

Other canal and dredging companies were formed, too, most of them in the South. The most famous was Virginia's Great Dismal Swamp Company, a project in which Washington was deeply interested. So was Colonel Light-Horse Harry Lee, who put all of his available funds into the project. This organization intended to drain the huge swamp, then grow rice and other crops in the rich soil. According to the ambitious plan, a canal was to be dug, connecting the Great Dismal Swamp with the Elizabeth River, in order to provide an outlet for the agricultural products. This company encountered many pitfalls, including financial mismanagement, and some investors, Lee among them, were wiped out. After a delay of years the canal was dug, the swamp was drained, and production was started. It might be noted that the entire project is in operation to the present day, precisely as it had been outlined by Washington and his associates.

One of the most successful ventures was the James River Company. Partly financed by the state of Virginia, it had as its object the improvement of navigation far into the interior along the James. This company paid its supporters handsomely.

In 1786, the South Carolina legislature charted a company to build a canal between the Santee and Cooper Rivers. The soft earth made the task formidable, but this canal was completed in 1800 and remained in operation until the eve of the Civil War, six decades later. Numbers of other schemes were projected in both South and North Carolina, but few were actually built.

The most renowned project in the North was the building of a bridge over the Charles River to connect Boston and Cambridge. The Massachusetts legislature issued a charter to a company for that purpose in 1785. The bridge was built the following year, and the entire scheme was a huge success from the outset. In fact, the company repaid the investors and made money for them so quickly that scores of other bridge companies came into being throughout the North.

Virtually all of them were profitable from the start. In fact, the country was growing so rapidly that, as Robert Morris said, it was almost impossible for these companies to fail. Although it is difficult to obtain accurate figures, a rough guess indicates that at least eight hundred bridges were constructed during the years of the Confederation.

It is equally difficult to estimate how many thousands of miles of roads came into being during the period. New York and Pennsylvania were the initial leaders, the legislatures of both states authorizing the building of new roads in 1783. Maryland and Connecticut followed a few months later, as did Virginia in mid-1784. But the officially authorized roads tell only a small part of the story.

So many immigrants were moving westward across the mountains that impatient trailblazers slashed the first roads through the forest. Those who came after them gradually improved these roads, broadening them, filling in holes, and digging up tree stumps. Most of the roads into the West were not planned projects. They were the result of necessity, and met the urge of the migrants to reach the frontier's free lands as quickly as they could.

Equally significant was the network of new roads that connected the older communities. Before the Constitution came into effect, mail was being carried by stagecoach all the way from the Maine district of Massachusetts to the more remote settlements of Georgia. "Civilization," said James Monroe, a young surveyor who would become his country's fifth President, "follows the roads that Americans are building everywhere. Soon our beloved wilderness may disappear."

The demand for carriages was so great that domestic companies began to build them for the first time. European manufacturers found it difficult to meet the tremendous American demand, and many would-be purchasers disliked paying the high European prices, not to mention the heavy cost of transporting the vehicles across the Atlantic.

The Boston *Gazette* estimated, in 1788, that the number of carriages in the country had tripled since the Battle of Yorktown. And everywhere, as the newspapers of the time show, people were voicing a familiar complaint: Traffic in the cities was becoming so congested that it was threatening American commercial life.

Obviously, the United States was suffering growing pains that, no matter how great the country's development, she did not enjoy.

VI. Foreign Relations

"We are a midget-like race," wrote United States Secretary of Foreign Affairs John Jay in 1786, "cast loose in a world inhabited by giants. We exist only at their pleasure, and our distance from Europe prevents us from being gobbled up alive by these rapacious monsters which possess appetites for other peoples and their lands, appetites which are insatiable."

The Atlantic was indeed a "protective moat," as John Adams called it, but the United States was growing so rapidly that the great empires of the world could not help casting covetous eyes at her. It was evident to every king and his ministers that a nation fortunate enough to obtain possession of the United States could become the most powerful on earth.

Desire for the reconquest of the lost colonies remained strong in Great Britain, where the Tory party still resented the nation's defeat by the upstart Americans. And the Tories were supported by a strong segment of British popular opinion.

It is hardly surprising that the British felt as they did. Their former colonies had been discovered, in the main, by Englishmen or mercenaries hired by the Crown. Englishmen had settled the better part of the land, developed it, and transferred English customs and institutions to it. And, as everyone was well aware, British subjects were still migrating to the New World in large numbers. The feeling of brotherhood that would emerge in Anglo-American relations was a century or more away. The relationship was still that between a parent and a rebellious child. From the English point of view, the tie, although strained, still existed between blood relatives.

The position of the French was complicated, too. The United States owed her very existence as an independent nation to France. Gold from the French treasury, French arms, supplies, and food, and the direct aid of the French army and navy had made it possible for the United States to win the war.

There was great admiration in France, particularly in educated circles, for the goals and aspirations of the infant democracy. Many of those who participated in the French Revolution that began in 1789 had grown to believe in the ideals embodied in the liberty the Americans had achieved. And the part played in the American Revolution by such prominent Frenchmen as the Marquis de Lafayette also had been effective in shaping the attitudes of the most powerful nation in continental Europe.

But the feelings of the French were ambivalent. Only about a decade before the Americans had started their fight for independence, France had lost a vitally important military struggle against the British in what the New World called the French and Indian Wars. In that struggle France had lost the heartland of her American empire, Canada, to Great Britain.

The humiliation still rankled, and there were millions in France who continued to regard Britain as the primary enemy. The entire nation yearned for the recovery of a New World empire, which had been the glory of France since the reign of Henry IV in the early seventeenth century.

Officials of the War and Navy Ministries in Paris well realized they lacked the strength to defeat the British in a new war. Great efforts were being made, in spite of the abysmal corruption and inefficiencies that riddled France in the reign of Louis XVI, to improve the strength of the armed services, but these efforts were not enough.

One way to defeat Britain, the classic way, would be to obtain the help of a strong ally. France did not know where to turn, however. The Dutch, in a major war, invariably sided with the English. So might the Austrians. Russia was too disorganized and corruption-ridden, hence too feeble to fight offensive wars. Of the major powers that left only Portugal, Britain's oldest and firmest friend in Europe, and Spain, which had her own fish to fry.

There was another way that France might achieve her goal, a way as obvious as it was simple. If she could gain control of the infant United States, that strength, added to her own, might ensure France a victory in a new, direct confrontation with Britain.

Help to the new nation had been given, in part, for this

selfish reason, and the French stood ready to collect the debt whenever they could. The United States was an ally, to be sure, but after their long war the Americans would not willingly plunge into another of their own free will.

Therefore France might be compelled to achieve by force of arms what she could not gain by diplomacy. Her army and navy, many government officials were convinced, certainly were strong enough to defeat the Americans. What was more, French generals and admirals, having served with the Americans, would know the weaknesses and the strengths of their wartime ally. A thorough study had been made of British mistakes in the American Revolution, too, and France would not repeat them if she became embroiled with the United States.

The idea of taking possession of the United States was appealing to French patriots for another, more compelling reason. If France became the ruler of the new nation, Great Britain might find her hold on sparsely settled, formerly French-owned Canada untenable. It was possible that England might even order the voluntary evacuation of her forces from the only two Canadian communities of any significant size: Quebec, the capital, and Montreal. If not, French forces pushing northward from the United States could, in coordinated attacks, drive the British out with relative ease.

The Americans were aware of the potential threat posed by the French. Franklin, as American Minister to France, had reported the feelings of this circle a number of times. Jefferson did the same from 1785 to 1789, the years he

was the American Minister in Paris. The United States
well understood that the conquest of her territory was
not the current policy of the King and his government.
But there was an ever-present danger: it was possible,
from week to week, even from day to day, that strong-
minded militarists might sweep into power in France.

A third menace to the young nation was posed by
Spain. No longer the formidable power she had been in
previous centuries, royal Spain was still strong enough to
do incalculable harm to the United States. Her army was
dispirited, it is true, and the soldiers she sent to her New
World colonies were poorly trained, badly paid, and in-
different to their duties. But her navy was still very strong,
commanded by competent, courageous officers, and
manned by efficient seamen. That navy could play havoc
with American shipping.

The Spanish threat had to be taken seriously also for
another reason. Spain was the largest European colonial
power in the entire New World. She controlled large portions of South America, at least nominally, and held more
islands in the West Indies than any other nation.

More to the point, she was the immediate neighbor of
the United States to the south and west. She owned the
Floridas, which lay south of Georgia, and the wilderness
territory that would become Alabama. She owned vast
stretches of territory west of the Mississippi.

Her claim to millions of square miles directly conflicted
with the claims of the United States. The border was ill
defined in many parts of the West, and much of the region had not been thoroughly explored, much less mapped

and surveyed. No American could forget, either, that Spain controlled the Mississippi River, which was the route to the sea for the American West. And the largest Spanish fort in the entire New World was located at New Orleans, the port city directly above the mouth of the Mississippi.

Conscious of her declining prestige, Spain was anxious to recoup some of the glory she had known in the past. She was too weak to wage aggressive war on any other European nation. But, with her bases throughout the Americas and her strong navy, she was tempted to attack the United States, drive her settlers out of the West, and take possession of the lands beyond the Appalachian Mountains. If this were to happen, the United States would be confined to the seaboard, condemned to become a small, impotent nation with no hope of expansion or growth.

There was even a chance that Spain might be able to achieve her goals without going to war. Many of the Americans migrating to the still sparsely settled West had no deep feelings of allegiance to the new United States. The young nation had not been in existence long enough for her people to sink their roots very deep. This was especially true of the immigrants. And large numbers of other settlers, particularly those in Kentucky and the Franklin district of North Carolina, felt they were being neglected and abused by both the states and the Confederation.

So Spain saw an opportunity to fan the flames of dis-affection. By paying hard cash to the settlers, making special commercial concessions to them in their Mississippi River trade, and, above all, by promising them self-government, she might be able to wean them away from the United States and cause them to proclaim their allegiance to Spain.

It must be remembered here that eighteenth-century American national feelings were not like those of later periods. Men were proud of their states, of course. But the Continental Congress had been a bumbling organization that had won the respect of no one. And the government of the Confederation inspired no strong loyalties, either. Consequently the Spaniards had good reason to hope they might be able to woo the men of the American West.

The feelings of Americans toward each of the three powers were complex. Great Britain, of course, inspired the deepest emotions, both of hate and of affection.

Many Americans despised the British with an abiding passion. Certainly this was true of many who had fought the Redcoats. It was equally true of the residents of New York, Newport, Charleston, and other communities that had been occupied by the British at one time or another during the war. There were tens of thousands, too, who had been influenced by the stories of "atrocities" and other anti-Redcoat propaganda written by such men as Sam Adams throughout the war. It did not matter that most of the tales of vile deeds allegedly committed by British and German mercenary troops were untrue, that they had as little basis in fact as other, similar stories circulated in other wars.

What mattered was that a hard core of American patriots was convinced the tales were true. This group included many members of the younger generation growing to manhood and womanhood during the war years. They knew nothing about the British except what they had learned during that period, and their feelings were bitter.

On the other hand, there were Americans who still felt ties of affection and even loyalty to England. These people were American patriots, too, but might be termed "reluctant patriots." They had dreaded the coming of the war, could see where both sides had been right and both wrong in many ways, and found it difficult to abandon everything that they had held dear all their lives.

Most historians are inclined to believe that this group comprised the majority of Americans. The war was fought and conducted by a tiny minority, some of whom were considered radicals. For example, the Continental Army was never able to muster more than a maximum strength of eleven thousand troops.

Even the men who signed the Declaration of Independence and other American leaders did not reject Great Britain. The correspondence and public statements of virtually all except Sam Adams and a handful of his fellow extreme radicals reveal that they looked upon Britons as brothers. All were descended from one common stock. All shared a heritage of political and personal freedom. All knew that the future of the United States depended upon the might of Britain, the world's strongest and foremost defender of the rights of man.

To be sure, they, too, had hated England during the war years. But, as so many of them wrote and said, these antipathies died away when the fighting was over. A natural sympathy and sense of understanding reasserted themselves. The situation very much resembled that of a family that may fight or feud, but is basically united in spite of its differences.

It is significant that this was the approach taken by all five of the first Presidents of the United States: Washington, John Adams, Jefferson, Madison, and Monroe. Other prominent Americans who shared these feelings and thoughts ranged from Benjamin Franklin to Alexander Hamilton. There were prominent exceptions, of course. John Hancock was one, and no one could blame him for his continuing hatred of the British. After all, a Crown order for his capture had been issued at the beginning of the war, and he would have been hanged had he been caught.

Certainly the American commercial interests favored a resumption of friendly ties with Great Britain. Merchants wanted to start trading again, as did shipowners and the Southern planters whose cotton and other products were sent to English mills and markets. English merchants and shipowners shared the feelings of their American counterparts and colleagues. Naturally, so did the mill owners who needed American products. Men who depended upon American lumber and furs for their living wanted a resumption of close relations as soon as possible, too.

These men, working on both sides of the Atlantic, exerted pressure on their governments. Their efforts were effective, and the treaty that ended the war in 1783 contained a special clause. A new commercial treaty, it said, should be arranged as soon as possible. This agreement would ease the commercial relations of the two countries, and would be based upon "mutual advantage and convenience."

In the meantime, it was agreed, informally, that there would be no tariff barriers to hinder trade. American goods would be allowed to enter Great Britain without paying any import taxes. British goods would be allowed to enter the United States freely. This arrangement went into effect immediately, and both countries benefited. In fact, by 1785, their volume of annual trade was actually greater than it had been at any time before the war.

Unfortunately for both nations, this happy situation did not last beyond the years of the Confederation. There were elements in Britain, well represented in Parliament, that still wanted to punish the former colonies for having seceded. They managed to obtain a number of new laws that severely hampered and cut down British-American trade relations. This damage was not undone until the two nations fought each other again in the so-called "second War of Independence," the War of 1812.

France took full advantage of her wartime friendship with the United States to improve trade relations with the new nation. French merchants looked forward to an increased market, since there were several million Americans who were potential good customers. In order to encourage trade, France was very generous. For example, seven major French ports in her West Indian colonies were opened to free American trade. This meant American merchants could sell codfish and other products to the French in the Caribbean without paying local taxes.

They could also, tax-free, obtain French colonial sugar, fruit, and tobacco.

"The French of the West Indies," the Pennsylvania *Gazette* gleefully reported in 1785, "are disposed to confer every favor upon Americans."

American merchants and shippers responded so energetically to this pleasant situation that French businessmen in the Caribbean, who were forced to pay taxes (Americans were not), were hurt. They lost a customer every time the Americans gained one. These West Indian merchants complained so loudly to Paris that the French government was forced to reverse its policies. The trade "honeymoon" of the two nations came to an end in 1787. In that year, import taxes were imposed on a wide variety of American products, including turpentine, whale oil, hides, furs, lumber, potash, flour, grains, and tar.

These restrictions did not halt the flow of trade, however. The Americans discovered illegal ways of doing what had been accomplished legally. The Caribbean became a vast smugglers' market, and American products were taken ashore at night, after the tax collectors had gone home for the day. As a matter of fact, American profits increased, because French buyers were willing to pay more for smuggled goods.

The hardheaded, shrewd Dutch showed the most realistic attitude. All through the war years the merchants and shippers of Holland had been looking forward to the establishment of trade relations with the United States. Peter van Berckel, the first Dutch Minister to the

United States, arrived in 1783 and immediately made a study of the trade situation. To the surprise of no one, the diplomat reported that an illegal trade already existed, and was harmful to the Dutch East India Company, the government-controlled trading organization.

Instead of trying to plug the loopholes and cut down smuggling, which would have been very difficult, the Dutch behaved very sensibly. Within six months the government extended a substantial trade loan to the United States. Dutch merchants were encouraged to make private loans on generous terms to struggling American merchants. They also offered American purchasers a wide variety of Dutch goods at special low prices.

As a result of these liberal policies, Dutch-American trade enjoyed a tremendous boom. Within two years, the Dutch East India Company, instead of losing money, was showing a handsome profit in the American market. Everyone on both sides benefited greatly.

Equally important, the basis was laid for a close Dutch-American friendship. That relationship has continued without interruption till today. The United States was able to return Holland's kindness in the years immediately following World War II. At that time American funds, both official and private, helped to put the war-shattered Dutch economy on its feet again.

One other small maritime nation, Sweden, showed similar foresight. The Swedish government also was anxious to initiate trade relations with the United States. In fact, she was so eager that, rather than handle the matter by slow trans-Atlantic mails, the Swedes sent a special mission to Paris.

This group was authorized to make a trade treaty with Benjamin Franklin, the American Minister to France, on any suitable terms. The delighted Franklin immediately communicated with the Confederation government, which promptly gave him a free hand to negotiate.

The treaty, the first commercial agreement in the short history of the young United States, was signed on April 3, 1783. Swedish-American trade started at once, and both countries enjoyed increased prosperity.

Two other treaties of commerce and friendship were signed in the next few years. One, with Prussia, was concluded in September, 1785. It, too, helped the American economy and gave American producers new and profitable markets. The other agreement, with Morocco, was signed in January, 1787. It proved to be no more than a token, except that it gave American merchant shipping convenient port bases in the Mediterranean. The Sultan of Morocco, like American officials, was seeking increased prestige for his country, and any treaties he could negotiate helped improve his country's standing.

In practical terms, however, this agreement was useless. And within a few years it proved a liability. By the early part of the following century, America was at war with the pirate states of North Africa. Morocco was sympathetic to her sister Barbary nations at that time, but did not break diplomatic relations with the United States. So the treaty remained in effect, at least in theory.

The new American nation plunged headlong into the world of international relations after achieving her independence. When Portugal knew she would not be punished by the British for her temerity, she opened negotiations with the United States. After years of conversations that extended beyond the period of the Confederation, she signed a trade treaty with the new nation.

Denmark, followed the example of Sweden, but took her time in leisurely talks. The Danes had no intention of losing business while the negotiations dragged on, however, and realistically established trade relations in the interim. She accepted American imports without duty taxes and extended the same courtesy in return. Therefore Danish-American relations proved to be remarkably similar to those achieved under the Swedish-American understanding.

Venice, the kingdom of the Two Sicilies, and the free port of Hamburg opened trade talks with the Americans, and these tiny maritime states eventually were able to work out treaties, too. Everywhere the United States received loans and easy credit terms that helped her grow more prosperous. In 1788, still another treaty was signed with the German principality of Saxony, but inadequate transportation facilities on both sides proved to be an obstacle. So this agreement did little to improve the trade situation of either.

There were dark spots as well as bright in the international relations of the United States. One of the worst concerned frontier outposts that the British, under the terms of the Treaty of Paris, promised to give up. These fortresses were strategically located, and by abandoning them the British would have weakened their hold on Canada. So they found excuses, all of them flimsy, to keep such places as Fort Detroit, Niagara, and Michilimackinac (Mackinac), on the Straits of Mackinac, which connects Lake Michigan and Lake Huron.

Americans deeply resented the continuing presence of Redcoats at these forts. And the British commanders on the scene made a number of blunders that further complicated the relations of the two countries. They refused American shippers the right to send their vessels into the Great Lakes, an order that was enforced by British gunboats. Even worse, they strengthened their own positions at the expense of the Americans by giving ammunition, money, and liquor to the Indian tribes of the West.

Certainly nothing could have made the American frontiersmen angrier. Whenever an American farm was raided or an American citizen shot by Indian raiders, British weapons, British ammunition, and British gunpowder were believed to have been used, regardless of whether the charge was true or not.

The United States was exceptionally fortunate in one respect. The men charged with the conduct of her foreign relations were of the highest caliber. In fact, some historians believe the nation has never been better represented. John Jay, who was Secretary of Foreign Affairs, was a man of lofty ideals and great talent. After the adoption of the Constitution, he became the first Chief Justice of the United States Supreme Court. John Adams was given the most difficult of all posts, that of Minister to Great Britain. His was the task of restoring normal relations with the former mother country, and he succeeded brilliantly. He performed with dogged persistence, soothing British tempers while serving the best interests of his own country at all times. In spite of countless difficulties, he achieved a smooth working relationship with the British.

Thomas Jefferson was Jay's inspired choice as Minister to France. If any man could take Franklin's place, that man was Jefferson, who was equally intellectual, equally polished, equally at home at a highly sophisticated court. Seldom in history has one genius appeared to fill the boots of another.

No matter how complicated her present and how threatening her future, America was being led by extraordinary men.

VII. The Industrial Revolution

The United States came of age in more ways than one in the era of the Confederation. If worthy of being remembered for nothing else, the years 1781–89 are significant because during that period the foundation was laid for the establishment of an industrial nation. Within a century and a half, the United States would become the most powerful and most successful industrial nation in the history of civilization.

Prior to the Revolution, the thirteen colonies and their frontier lands had been almost exclusively agricultural. The British New World posessions had existed for the sole purpose of providing the mother country with raw materials. This, at least, was the opinion of a succession of Crown governments.

Certain types of factories and plants were specifically forbidden by law in the colonies. The colonists were not allowed to establish or operate iron foundries, nor could they manufacture metal products of any kind. They could not make their own frying pans, kettles, and kitchen utensils. All such items had to be imported. This meant, for all practical purposes, that they were purchased in Great Britain.

The coming of the war abruptly ended the flow of manufactured goods to the United States. This left Americans with two alternatives: They could buy what they needed elsewhere, or they could manufacture their own products. The effectiveness of the British naval embargo, combined with the extreme poverty of Americans, soon narrowed the choice.

The first iron foundry was built at Worcester, a little town on the Massachusetts frontier. By the end of the war, the country boasted a dozen foundries in all—several in New England, two in Delaware, and one each in Pennsylvania, Maryland, and New York. And by 1786, according to an admittedly incomplete economic survey that Jefferson made while in France, there were seven plants making finished iron products operating in the United States, with three others in the process of being built.

Nothing, perhaps, had irritated the American colonists as much, prior to 1775, as a British law that prohibited them from constructing and operating mills of any kind that manufactured cloth. The purpose of this statute, of course, was the protection of British mills, which sold vast quantities of wool and other cloth to the colonies.

The law did not apply to home spinners and weavers, so American women by the thousands made linen and wool under their own roofs. But their efforts were not sufficient to meet the demands of a nation. During the early years of the war there was an acute shortage of wool in the United States; none could be obtained except what was smuggled into the country from the Dutch West Indies. Later in the war, France supplied bolts of cloth.

At the war's end, British manufacturers hoped and planned to regain their American markets. But a number of enterprising Americans thought otherwise. Raw wool was exported to Great Britain in quantity. Flax was grown on hundreds, perhaps thousands, of American farms. And the cotton of the American South was already replacing that of India as the primary source of cotton cloth, or Madras, as it was commonly known. There was no good reason, Americans thought, why they should not establish their own cloth-manufacturing mills.

Conditions were best suited to this purpose in New England. There were more fairly heavily populated towns in the area, so a labor force was available. Waterpower, which was essential to mill operations, was plentiful and good. And, through sheer good fortune, a large number of expert mill workers were among the first postwar immigrants from the British Isles to come to the United States.

The first mills were established in 1784. Jefferson's figures estimate that three or four were built in that year. By 1786, there were at least forty-six in New England. The number was growing so swiftly that the disapproving Jefferson, who wanted America to remain an agricultural nation, said he thought the number would at least double again within the next decade.

American beaver pelts were in great demand throughout the civilized world, the skins being used to make hats for both ladies and gentlemen. Again, necessity forced Americans to develop new industries of their own. Previously the pelts had been exported, and all hats had been made abroad. Now, almost overnight, Americans became the world's largest makers of beaver hats. By 1789, they manufactured more than 90 percent of the world's beaver headgear. This industry served the vital function of bringing badly needed foreign funds into the United States.

Heavy industry had its actual beginnings during the war. Americans desperately needed arms and ammunition, and a few small, special foundries began the casting of cannon. These weapons, as Major General Henry Knox, Washington's artillery chief, soon discovered, were inferior and unreliable. They were difficult to aim, and more often than not exploded after firing a few rounds. After the war, however, these plants turned to the manufacture of rifles, pistols, and, to a limited degree, old-fashioned muskets.

Every man who went west to the frontier needed firearms. By 1787, the bulk of these weapons was being made by American manufacturers. Their products were not in a class with those manufactured in Great Britain or on the European continent, to be sure, but they had one natural advantage: They cost the poor immigrant or American townsman who was headed for the wilderness only a small fraction of what he would have paid for an imported weapon.

Several gunpowder plants sprang up, too, seemingly out of nowhere. Large quantities of saltpeter, which was needed for the making of powder, were available in

Delaware, which quickly became the center of the growing munitions industry.

Many prominent citizens went into business after the war. Major General Nathanael Greene, the second-ranking officer in the Continental Army, retired to an estate that the grateful state of Georgia gave him. But he was too active and energetic a man to spend the rest of his days in the country. He invested his money in a company that refined natural salt and manufactured rum, and spent much of his time supervising the organization.

The paint industry came into being, and soon was centered in Philadelphia. By 1785, according to the Pennsylvania *Gazette*, purchasers of household and other paint could buy it in eleven different colors from five prospering companies.

The nail business also grew rapidly out of nowhere. Until the war's end, not a single nail had been manufactured in the United States. Ever since the beginning of the war, individuals, principally farmers, had been using scraps of iron and other metal to make their own nails. The effort had been tedious, the results imperfect, and wry jokes about inferior nails were common. In 1784, a nail manufacturing company came into existence in New York, buying its raw materials from American foundries. Business was so overwhelming that by the following year three more nail-producing companies had been established.

Even shoes had been imported before the war, and by 1776 the supplies of merchants were exhausted. Thereafter, until 1783, it was almost impossible to buy a pair of shoes or boots anywhere in the United States. British shoemakers assumed they would be able to recapture their American markets at the end of the war, and, to an extent, they did. But several men in Massachusetts had other ideas.

A number of artisans who were master shoe- and boot-makers were among the early postwar immigrants. Domestic hides were inexpensive. In fact, many American hides previously had crossed the Atlantic, only to return as finished products. There seemed to be no good reason why Americans shouldn't make their own boots and shoes. In the middle of 1783, several companies were organized —two in Boston, one in Worcester, and another in frontier Springfield, where several shoemakers had just settled.

The need of the American public for new shoes was desperate. At the outbreak of war in 1775, a pair of fine ladies' shoes sold for $1.25, a pair of stout men's shoes for $1.00. Late in 1782, shoes of any kind smuggled in from the Dutch West Indies cost more than $5.00. This was an outrageous price when it is remembered that a skilled mason or carpenter, the most highly paid of artisans, earned less than $5.00 per week.

When the new companies began producing, shoe sales skyrocketed. Shopkeepers could not keep their merchandise in stock, and soon the manufacturers received orders that kept them busy for months ahead. The boom created attention in business circles, naturally, and so many former Continental officers from Massachusetts regiments opened their own small factories that the New Haven *Gazette* jokingly suggested that they adopt a boot, thread, and needle as the insignia of their units.

The demand for experienced craftsmen in the growing industry became so great that two groups sent letters to John Adams in London, in 1785, asking him to recruit on their behalf. Of course, he could not do this, since it would have injured his dignity as a diplomat. So, in the following year, the Massachusetts shoe men sent their own agent to tour Great Britain. He offered high wages, bonuses, and other inducements to master shoemakers if they would migrate to the United States.

Fragments of correspondence indicate that his journey was successful, although no figures are available to show how many masters he could persuade to leave England for greener pastures. It is known, however, that the shoemakers of the United States drastically revised their standards. In 1786, the masters decided to promote apprentices after they had served only two years instead of the traditional seven. Then they were journeymen shoemakers for only two years more, cutting five additional years from their training before they, too, became masters.

Before the period of the Confederation came to an end, Massachusetts was making more than 70 percent of America's shoes. The Southern states in particular were buying from the New Englanders. And the newspapers proudly predicted that the country soon would become self-sufficient in shoemaking.

According to the Massachusetts *Centinel,* a factory was established somewhere in New Hampshire, in late 1785, for the making of buttons and thread. And a few months later, the New Haven *Gazette* proudly reported that 160,000 silkworms had been raised in Connecticut that spring. Some Pennsylvanians tried raising silkworms,

too, but enjoyed far less success. Pennsylvanians also
tried to set up cotton mills, but encountered too many
difficulties.

James Wilson, who as a boy had migrated from Scotland to Pennsylvania, and who later became an Associate
Justice of the United States Supreme Court, was responsible for one of the most ambitious industrial projects
in the country. He and several associates purchased a
site of ten thousand acres on the Delaware River, near
Philadelphia. There they intended to build a huge iron-
finishing plant that would employ several hundred men.
They had the staggering sum of $400,000 in hand, in
British pound sterling, and believed they required an
additional $250,000 in order to make the plant operable.

Peter van Berckel, the Dutch Minister, became interested in the scheme, and a number of Dutch bankers,
at his instigation, agreed to put up part of the money.
Wilson sought the rest from old friends in Scotland and
England, but they took a long time making up their minds.

Meanwhile, Wilson and his friends put their ready
cash into other projects, so the ambitious plan languished.
Eventually the land was sold, but two of Wilson's associates, many years later, were among the partners in one
of the first iron-processing plants to be built at Pittsburgh, which became the leading steel-manufacturing
center in the United States.

So many women were operating spinning wheels in
their homes that parts and accessories were required for
them. Their manufacture became a major industry, too,
which was centered in Philadelphia. In 1787, a single
manufacturing shop sold 2,412 spinning-wheel irons in

a single year; each wheel took one man a full day to produce.

The postwar thirst for news and knowledge was so great throughout America that scores of newspapers and magazines were founded during the period of the Confederation. Benjamin Franklin's associates in Philadelphia had hoped to make presses that would fulfill domestic printing needs, but they soon found their ambitions were unrealistic. The task was laborious, their own equipment inadequate for such heavy manufacturing, and the demand overwhelmed them. Therefore, most presses were purchased in England and the German principalities.

Wood, the basic ingredient in the making of paper, was available in limitless supply, however. Paper mills were built in all thirteen states, and by the time the era of the Confederation came to an end, the United States was producing all of its own paper for the printing of books, newspapers, and magazines. In fact, the paper was of such superior quality and was made so inexpensively that quantities were being exported to Europe before the end of the century. The papermakers were the first American manufacturers to send their merchandise abroad on a large scale.

Glassmaking was the oldest of American industries. The Virginians at Jamestown had a small plant in 1608, built under the supervision of Captain John Smith. And the Pilgrims of Plymouth also started making glass, establishing their tiny plant in 1621, the year after their arrival in the New World. Most of the glass manufacturing was centered in the vicinity of Philadelphia, and all the larger plants were located there. Only during the wartime occupation of the city by General Howe and his successor, General Clinton, was the production of glass interrupted.

It was difficult to transport glass to the frontier settlements without shattering it, so a glassmaking industry was established in Kentucky in 1784. That was the beginning of a small boom in Kentucky. Within a year or two, enterprising citizens there were making many items that the pioneers of the West needed. It has been estimated that progress was so rapid that by 1789 Kentucky was manufacturing more than New York had produced as recently as 1765.

What the eighteenth century called the useful arts came into their own during the years of the Confederation. Tiles and pottery, ornamental iron, stoneware, and "fancy bricks" were produced in quantity. American cabinetmakers turned out handsome furniture. Silversmiths copied the work of the gifted Paul Revere of Boston. Many items of pewter, lead, brass, and copper were made by men with skilled hands and artistic, imaginative minds. Beautiful saddles were made by leather workers. Ships that were pleasing to the eye as well as seaworthy were built.

Few accomplishments gave Americans as much of a sense of pride in their country as the development of the "useful arts." Truly skilled craftsmanship had been a monopoly of the Old World, where men worked for a decade and a half as apprentices and journeymen before becoming masters. Americans, pressed by the demand for goods of all kinds, invented new tools that cut the manufacturing time, and made it possible for men with less exacting training to do good work. Many American products of the period have survived the test of the centuries, and today are judged the equal of the best produced in Europe.

"Our people," wrote the elderly Benjamin Franklin in 1787, "have a zeal and a natural talent for the manufacturing of fine and ornamental objects and goods that I have discovered in the men of no other nation. Master craftsmen who reap the rewards of their own labor flourish in our free and liberty-loving society as they flourish in no other place that I have seen."

New England began to produce fish oil for use in lamps, for cooking, and other purposes. Stockings for men, women, and children were manufactured in Connecticut and Rhode Island, and a substantial glove-making industry grew up in New York. Plows and other farming tools were turned out in large quantities by New Yorkers, and by the end of the Confederation period few farm implements were being imported from Great Britain and the continent of Europe.

The making of candles and soap remained a home industry for many years. Virtually every household made its own, and there was little demand for either item in the shops. It was the custom for this chore to be performed by the young daughters of a family. By the time they were six or seven years old, girls usually were familiar with the whole process of boiling fats for this purpose.

The cultivation of tobacco had been important in the South, particularly in Virginia and North Carolina, ever since the early seventeenth century. In fact, the systematic and scientific growing of tobacco had been started by John Rolfe, the husband of the Indian princess Pocahontas. Until the war, tobacco had been sent to England for the making of snuff, *segaros,* and pipe tobacco. But Americans quickly discovered they could do equally well on their own. New manufacturing equipment was invented by ingenious growers. And during the Confederation years the making of tobacco products became the largest and most important industry in both Virginia and North Carolina. A few plants were also established in Connecticut, where the soil and climate were found right for the growing of some of the more hardy types of tobacco.

Without exception, the factories established for the manufacture of all the different types of goods made in the United States were very small. By British standards, where a hundred or more persons might be employed in a single plant, they were laughable. An average American factory rarely employed more than ten persons, most of them sons or other relatives of the owner. In 1786, Alexander Hamilton estimated that the average plant in New York employed approximately five persons. Child labor was common, as it was in Europe. Two of the five persons employed in each plant or factory were usually under sixteen years of age.

The ingenuity of the infant nation was taxed to its utmost in acquiring tools and equipment for manufacture. For example, two machines were imported from England for carding and spinning when it was decided to start a cotton-manufacturing industry. The men who imported this machinery generously allowed others to examine and copy it. Several young Americans promptly went to work improving the machinery. Within a few years, Americans were using their own machinery for making cotton, and it was machinery superior to that used in England!

Undoubtedly, the largest single American industry was shipbuilding. The future of the new nation depended upon her trade with Europe and the West Indies. The demand for new merchant ships, with cabins for passengers, was so great that shipyards opened at a rapid rate in every seaport. The largest, of course, were located in the cities and bigger towns. But even small towns had their booming boatyards.

Naval architects were able to name their own fees for the designing of ships; it was customary for the designer to supervise the building of a new vessel. Carpenters who knew how to build ships were among the highest-paid artisans in the United States. For example, there had been a busy fishing-boat-manufacturing industry in Marblehead, Massachusetts, before the war. During the war, many of the carpenters and other craftsmen had served with great distinction in the regiment commanded by Colonel John Glover, a resident of the town. But during the 1780's, the Marbleheaders were hired by yards in Boston, Providence, Newport, New London, New Haven, and other New England cities. They worked as yard supervisors and earned wages three to five times greater than they had been paid before the war. In fact, it was said in Marblehead that there would have been no American shipbuilding industry without the Marbleheaders.

The handling of credit and other aspects of finance in a land where industry was mushrooming made it inevitable that new banks be founded in the United States. Throughout the colonial era and the war years, there had been no banks of any kind in the country. All banking was done in England, but some of the wealthier merchants in Boston, Philadelphia, and other cities loaned money on an informal basis.

When the war had ended, manufacturing started again, and with trade growing so rapidly, the need for American-owned, American-based banks became imperative. The imaginative Robert Morris founded the Bank of North America in 1781, buying much of its stock himself. One of his principal partners was William Duer, another Philadelphia merchant, who was his close friend.

The difficulties the Bank of North America encountered in its early days indicate the primitive nature of society in the infant nation. Morris, who was a member of the Continental Congress and was the chairman of its finance committee, persuaded his fellow delegates to borrow silver from France so the bank could operate. So Congress solemnly voted in favor of obtaining the specie, and Benjamin Franklin, then in Paris, arranged the loan.

The Bank was a private institution, of course. But it loaned money to the Confederation government, which had obtained the funds from France in the first place. It is small wonder that the affairs of the Bank were muddled during its first years.

It was a solid and profitable operation from the start, however. It loaned money to private companies and individuals as well as to the Confederation government, and the officers of the organization were prudent, far-seeing men. Among the directors were Gouverneur Morris and James Wilson of Philadelphia, both of them cautious, and the conservative Jeremiah Wadsworth of Connecticut, who eventually became the largest single stockholder.

By the middle of 1783, the Bank of North America was paying a dividend of 6½ percent to its stockholders. Others, including European bankers, wanted to invest, but none of the stockholders were willing to sell any of their holdings. This led the merchants of New York and Boston to wonder why they shouldn't form banks of their own and share in the new wealth.

Bank of North America directors wanted no competition that might cut down their own profits. So they cannily expanded their own company and issued additional shares of stock. These were purchased, almost literally overnight, by men in Boston and New York, as well as by representatives of various European banking interests. Talk of forming new banks temporarily faded away, and the Bank of North America continued to earn handsome profits for its investors.

In time, the pressures became too great to resist, and the merchants of Boston, led by the ever busy John Hancock, founded the Bank of Massachusetts in the late spring of 1784. At about the same time, in New York, Robert R. Livingston petitioned the state legislature for the right to start a bank, with one third of its shares to be paid in cash, the rest to be guaranteed by mortgages on lands in New York and New Jersey. Alexander Hamilton and his brother-in-law, John B. Church, joined forces with Livingston, but the members of the legislature balked. Most of them were farmers who instinctively suspected all banks of wanting to cheat them, and they refused to issue a charter.

Hamilton, who was far more daring than Livingston, became the prime mover in the attempt to organize a bank in New York. It occurred to him that the state's law was vague, and that no authorization by the legislature actually was needed to found a bank. In other words, he and his friends, if they chose, could thumb their noses at the state. The man who in a few years would become the first United States Secretary of the Treasury decided to go ahead.

A number of eager New York merchants were willing to share in the gamble, and bought stock. The Bank of New York opened its doors in June, 1784. It was a success from the start and its directors and officers exercised great care in their management of the institution.

By the 1790's, the defiance of New York was forgotten, and the state began to work closely with the Bank in the development of its own projects. Of all the early banks in the United States, the Bank of New York is the only one that has survived to the present day. It is still in operation, still doing business.

This continuing success is due, at least in part, to the refusal of the original directors to become involved in get-rich-quick land schemes. Robert Morris, Duer, and some of the other Bank of North America directors borrowed huge sums from that institution in order to buy vast tracts of land in the West, which they hoped to sell at a huge profit. But settlers moved instead into free lands, Morris and Duer went bankrupt, and the Bank of North America was badly crippled.

The Bank of Massachusetts narrowly escaped a similar fate. It remained conservative, however, and, confining itself to relatively small operations, stayed in business for many years before merging with newer organizations. Even in the late eighteenth and early nineteenth centuries, Boston was content with her position as the center of New England and, unlike New York and Philadelphia, did not aspire to a permanent first place among American cities.

In spite of the growth of American industry and banking during the years of the Confederation, the United States was still, above all, an agricultural nation. Her real prosperity was based, in the main, on her surplus crops. And Thomas Jefferson, who hoped she would always be a nation of farmers, had valid reasons for feeling as he did. The profits earned by farmers for their produce provided the funds that enabled cities to grow, industries to expand, huge networks of transportation facilities to come into being.

The greatest development in agriculture took place in the South in the years immediately following the war. Cotton and tobacco already had proved themselves profitable, and thousands of Northerners moved into undeveloped areas of Virginia, the Carolinas, and Georgia, as well as their frontier hinterlands.

The gains in tobacco growing were spectacular. The wilderness lands of western Georgia and South Carolina were settled by tobacco farmers, and tobacco also became the principal crop in many counties of Kentucky and Tennessee. American tobacco exports in 1781–89 increased almost 50 percent over the volume in the decade before the war, and the price of tobacco had risen 20 to 40 percent since that time. In other words, tobacco growing may well have been the most profitable of all American enterprises.

Indigo-plant growing also enjoyed a tremendous boom, particularly in South Carolina. The plant was used as the base for a cloth dye, and the product from South Carolina had been much in demand before the war. But it had not been grown according to scientific methods, the plant itself was very delicate, and the output was uncertain. Then, in 1783, General Francis Marion came home from the war, and went to work on his South Carolina farm to develop a new type of indigo. The strain he produced was hardy, required little care, and flourished in the South Carolina climate. Marion patriotically gave indigo plants to his neighbors, relatives, and friends, and within a year more than forty thousand acres of it had been planted.

By 1785, indigo became South Carolina's principal export, and the state ranked first among the world's producers of the dye. It held that position for more than thirty years. In the 1790's, Great Britain tried to lessen her dependence on South Carolina indigo by encouraging planters in the West Indies to grow it. They did, but their strain was inferior, and the demand for the South Carolina plant remained heavy until the 1830's, when new dyes that could be manufactured less expensively began to appear on the world markets.

England's appetite for cotton during the years of the

Confederation led to the spectacular growth of cotton exports. New machinery developed in England around 1770 enabled manufacturers there to quadruple their output of cotton cloth, but the coming of the war cut off the source of raw material. In the early 1780's, the Americans were using crude but effective cotton gins that enabled them to export a superior brand of cotton. It should be noted that these gins were in use more than a decade before Eli Whitney invented his improved cotton gin in 1793.

Cotton was in such demand in England, France, and the German principalities that Virginia and North Carolina encouraged their farmers to grow it in place of tobacco. In 1786, the Virginia legislature debated a bill that proposed placing a tax on tobacco growing, and using the revenue to pay a bonus to farmers who grew cotton. The idea was so radical that nothing came of the measure.

But the South needed no prodding from state legislatures to produce cotton. The clamor for it was so great that farmers throughout the area naturally turned to it. In 1785, for example, South Carolina and Georgia grew an estimated two million pounds for domestic use and exported approximately the same amount. This activity laid the groundwork for the enthronement of "King Cotton" in the South. In 1801, over eight million pounds were exported from Charleston alone, and the produce for domestic consumption was more than ten million pounds.

As a general rule, cotton was grown on large plantations, and the small farmers of the back country produced wheat and corn, along with a smattering of oats and rye. In the years before the Revolution, the Middle Atlantic colonies had been the breadbasket of the country, but the emphasis shifted during the years of the Confederation, and the small farmer of the South took first place.

Southern farmers grew far more grain than was needed for domestic purposes. By 1789, the South produced approximately two thirds of the corn and wheat exported from the United States. And the previously sleepy town of Alexandria, Virginia, became one of the grain seaports of the world.

The Middle Atlantic states still continued to produce grain, although their share of the market was dwindling. Only New England completely lost her standing as a grain-producing area. In the years prior to the war, she had grown enough for her own needs. But the sharp increase in her population, the poor soil, and the small size of her farms forced her to depend more on other parts of the country. By 1785, she was compelled to buy most of her grain in New York and Pennsylvania.

Dairy farming, oddly, expanded in New England. Although it was economically unsound for the New England farmer to grow corn or wheat in quantity, every farm supported a number of cows and chickens. In 1784, the region took first place as an exporter of butter and cheese, which were sent in bulk to Great Britain, Venice, and the German states. There was also a great demand in Europe for a New England delicacy: roasted eggs that had been cooked in slow-burning maple charcoal.

The Middle Atlantic states took first place in the pro-

duction of meat. Beef and pork were exported to Great
Britain and Europe in quantity, usually smoked. And
there was an insatiable demand for venison, which the
hunters of the frontier could not meet in spite of high
prices.

One of the most significant aspects of American farming during the era of the Confederation was the newly
awakened interest in scientific methods of agriculture.
This interest was matched by a similar awakening in
Europe, and the intellectuals of both continents cor-
responded regularly on the subject.

In the United States, the lead was taken by the American Philosophical Society and the American Academy
of Arts and Sciences. The former was concerned, in the
main, with the broader aspects of scientific farming. It
paid farmers to experiment with new crops and cross-
breeding, and published papers on the results of these
efforts. In 1787, it offered a prize for the most effective
fertilizer developed by an American farmer. And in 1788,
it took charge of an experimental silkworm farm.

The Society also encouraged prospectors to search
for all kinds of mineral deposits. This effort led directly
to the finding of coal and iron in parts of Pennsylvania
and the portion of Virginia that later became West
Virginia.

The members of the Society were conscious of the
great weakness of American farming—inadequate transportation facilities. Farmers who grew bumper crops frequently went bankrupt because they had no way of
moving their produce to markets. Often there were no
roads; at best, there were only narrow trails. Wagons

were small. Waterways often did not connect, and small riverboats could not carry large quantities of grain, cotton, and tobacco.

So the Society helped various men who were trying to develop a new type of watercraft called the steamboat. Society members worked with the inventors of sturdier wagons and coaches, and the Society officially sponsored programs calling for the construction of canals that would link the major inland waterways.

The Academy was more specific in its investigations. Learning about the principles of crop rotation being tried in Europe, it paid farmers in New England, the Middle Atlantic States, and the South to try various combinations of rotating their crops. A number of Academy members conducted exhaustive experiments of their own in the hope of finding ways to preserve pork and beef exported to the West Indies. Eventually they found a number of ways to preserve meat for longer periods in tropical climates.

The Academy became interested in tobacco, and encouraged farmers to experiment with different types of tobacco plants in different soils and climates. And, at an experimental station of their own near Boston, eight Academy members personally tried their hand at growing carrots. Until the period of the Confederation, only wild carrots were found anywhere in the United States. Before the experiments ended in 1788, the carrot was domesticated and economical ways of growing lettuce, beans, and other vegetables had been developed. This proved to be a great boon to the small New England farmer who was able to grow crops.

Societies for the promotion of agriculture were formed in every state but New York by the mid-1780's. These organizations, usually made up of wealthy gentlemen farmers and planters, offered prizes for successful crop-rotation programs and methods of curtailing insects and other pests that destroyed cotton, tobacco, grains, and vegetables.

Competition for these prizes was keen, but the results were rather poorly publicized, so news of developments spread slowly. And frontier farmers paid virtually no attention to discoveries in scientific farming. They were so busy making homes for their families in the wilderness and fighting off Indians that things like the principles of crop rotation meant nothing to them. Unfortunately, the majority of Westerners remained poor for many years, and more than a quarter of a century would pass before the frontiersman took advantage of what farmers in the older, more established sections of the country already had learned.

VIII. A United People

"We are a frugal people, hard-working, honest and full of good cheer for our future. When our whale fishers suffer a bad season, our cod fishers bring in their largest catches. When a tobacco crop fails, cotton more than makes up the difference. When a paper mill goes bankrupt, its owner makes his fortune in cloth. How can such a people fail to become great?"

These were the words of optimism expressed by Benjamin Franklin when he returned to Philadelphia in September, 1785, after spending more than nine years abroad. The occasion was a great one, and the entire city joined in the celebration. A company of Philadelphia cavalry in full-dress uniform escorted the great man to his house. Whistles blew on board the ships tied up at the wharves. Ornamental cannon that had not been used since the end of the war were dusted off and fired. And every church bell in Philadelphia rang out.

Franklin, although almost eighty years of age, was a shrewd observer, and was heartened by everything he saw. His confidence in the political future of the United States was boundless. To a friend in London, he wrote:

> We are conducting the first experiment in self-government ever launched by any people. Since we have no guides to lead us through the political wilderness, I do not become disheartened when, upon occasion, we stumble and fall. Always we pull ourselves to our feet again, wipe away the mud and march on, undaunted. It does not impress itself upon me that we are the only people who have set up a new institution of government in accordance with a philosophical ideal. Attempts have been made by other peoples at other times in the long History of Man. What does impress itself upon me is that we, alone of all nations, are achieving success in our experiment. We have navigated the shoals, and albeit the seas in which we currently sail are storm-tossed, clear sailing lies ahead. We soon shall make necessary adjustments in our form of government, in order to make the form more perfect.
>
> I so predict because our people demand perfection. They will accept no less, and I find it remarkable that any people with so little experience in the art of governing can move with such certain steps toward inevitable improvements in the governing of themselves.

Franklin was scornful of the attitude taken toward the United States by the British press. In letter after letter to his friends and acquaintances in England, he cautioned against giving heed to anything printed by the "lying newspapers." The press, he said, was publishing what it thought the people of Britain wanted to hear about America, but little of it was true. He was willing to grant that prices were high, that there was conflict between city dwellers and farmers, and that every legislator considered himself the ultimate political expert, capable of revising the American governmental system.

These difficulties, he said, were minor symptoms, no more than growing pains. The United States was not only on the right political road, he said, but was enjoying a degree of prosperity he could not have visualized. The country's produce was abundant, and excellent prices were being paid for it both at home and abroad. There was no unemployment, and workmen in every trade and field enjoyed the best wages in history. The prices of land and houses in the settled areas were soaring, and property was worth more than three times what it had been before the war. Those values, incidentally, would continue to increase, and would double again within the next four years.

The status of American commerce delighted Franklin. British merchants no longer had a monopoly, and Americans were able to import any goods they needed, from any one of a dozen lands. He wrote to a friend in France:

> We are as comfortably situated as you in Paris and Marek in Amsterdam. We order what we fancy, through the good offices of our merchants and shopkeepers, and the prices we pay for merchandise of all natures is far less dear than it was when we lived under British rule, at the mercy of greedy British merchants.

What amazed the returning diplomat more than anything else he saw was the number of new buildings in the cities. The appearance of Philadelphia in particular startled him. After all, he said in several letters, the city was his home and should have been familiar to him "in all of its aspects." But there were so many new houses, shops, wharves, office buildings, schools, public meeting halls, churches, college buildings, and other structures that he wandered through the streets bemused and lost, like an immigrant newly arrived from some distant land.

Franklin was his usual canny self in his appraisal of the new nation's foreign situation. He unburdened himself in a letter to the Marquis de Lafayette, the young French nobleman who had fought so valiantly to help the United States win her independence. Lafayette had just written at some length, expressing his concern over the contempt for America that was evident in British ruling circles. Franklin calmly advised him not to worry about the attitudes of the new nation's former enemies.

"Let them think us weak, confused and friendless," he wrote, "so that they may then not be jealous of our growing strength, which, since the peace, does really make rapid progress."

Another optimist was Charles Thomson, who had become secretary of the Continental Congress before the war, and held the same position during the Confederation period. Writing to Thomas Jefferson in Paris in 1786, he painted a glowing picture of the state of the nation:

> I venture to assert there is not upon the face of the earth
> a body of people more happy or rising into consequence
> with more rapid strides than the inhabitants of the

United States of America. Population is increasing, new houses building, new lands clearing, new settlements forming, and new manufactures establishing with a rapidity beyond conception, and what is more, the people are well clad, well fed and well housed.

A cooler analysis was made by General Washington, who viewed every situation dispassionately and refused to let himself become emotionally involved. In a letter to another of the French volunteers, the wartime commander in chief wrote that he was unhappy because the states had recently refused to grant the Continental Congress the right to establish national tariffs and regulate the country's international trade. This, he said, could be harmful to America when the economic boom ended.

However, he added,

> . . . our internal governments are daily acquiring strength. The laws have their fullest energy; justice is well administered; robbery, violence or murder are not heard of from New Hampshire to Georgia. The people at large, as far as I can learn, are more industrious than they were before the war. Economy begins, partly from necessity and partly from choice and habit, to prevail. The seeds of population are scattered over an immense tract of western country. In the old states, which were the theatres of hostility, it is wonderful to see how soon the ravages of war are repaired. Houses are rebuilt, fields enclosed, stocks of cattle which were destroyed are replaced, and many a desolate territory assumes again the cheerful appearance of cultivation. In many places the vestiges of conflagration and ruin are hardly to be traced. The arts of peace, such as clearing rivers, building bridges, and establishing conveniences for traveling &c.

are assiduously promoted. In short, the foundation of a
great empire is laid, and I please myself with a persuasion, that Providence will not leave its work imperfect.

Washington's portrait of America's future was surpris-
ingly accurate. This is particularly interesting when it is
remembered that he spent virtually all his time at his
plantation in Virginia, rarely visiting the cities or doing
other traveling. It has been suggested that he kept in
touch with most of what was taking place throughout
the country by corresponding with friends and former
subordinate officers. Certainly it is true that many visitors
came to his home at Mount Vernon and there dis-
cussed affairs of the day with him.

Whatever his sources of information, Washington had
a clear picture of the world in which he lived. He also
formed and retained a vision of the America that generations yet to come would inherit. Of all Americans,
perhaps, the man who would become the first President
under the Constitution in 1789 best understood the great
destiny that awaited the United States.

The patrician Robert R. Livingston of New York lacked
Washington's ability to sense the shape of the future,
but he was even more hardheaded and realistic. An un-
enthusiastic supporter of the Revolution in 1775, he had
very much doubted that the rabble of the New World
would prevail over the forces representing law, tradi-
tion, and order.

Gradually, almost in spite of himself, Livingston became a patriot who believed in his country, while, at
the same time, remaining sensitive to her faults. He was
one of the first men of the age to realize that the Con-

federation was too weak to cope with the problems of a bustling, growing nation. He saw that something had to be done to strengthen the national government, especially in the fields of foreign affairs, fiscal policies, tax collection, international trade, defense, and immigration. He also knew there was a need for a national government with sufficient authority to settle disputes between the states.

At the same time, however, he was delighted by the progress the country was making, and was stunned by the speed of New York's recovery after years of enemy occupation. The population of the city soared, and that of the state as a whole almost doubled. Trade, both domestic and foreign, was booming. New buildings were being erected at a dizzy rate, a symbol of the growth New York would continue to demonstrate in the future. He complained that it was difficult to hire artisans at wages less than outrageous. But, in the same breath, he happily admitted that the high wages were criteria of unprecedented prosperity that made it impossible for him to doubt the ultimate success of the American experiment.

The major newspapers of the United States were also critical of the Confederation's weakness. The national government was almost impotent, the Pennsylvania *Gazette* said repeatedly, beginning in 1785. The interests of the individual states were selfish, their outlook limited. A few states, acting together, could block moves that would be of benefit to the entire nation.

Obviously this was wrong. Something had to be done, and the *Gazette*'s editorials expressed the conviction that whatever was necessary would be accomplished. This approach by the newspaper is worthy of further, close examination.

The *Gazette*'s attitude was far from unique or unusual. On the contrary, it seemed typical of the entire United States. The many in all walks of life who knew that the Confederation was inadequate and that it was necessary to devise a better form of government showed little bitterness or anger. Men everywhere took it for granted that the governmental system would be revised. There seemed to be no question about it in their minds.

They disagreed completely with their opponents, those who felt that all power should be kept in the hands of the states. But there was little heat in the arguments of the national-government advocates. Certainly there was nothing personal in their debates.

The same was true of the states'-rights men. The very principles on which the United States was founded, they believed, would be destroyed if the national government were strengthened at the expense of the states. So, although they, too, felt that their foes were misguided and shortsighted, the states'-rights men also kept their tempers.

This mutual regard indicated something significant in the attitude of all Americans. Everyone, no matter what his own convictions, accepted as a basic fact of life that everyone else, no matter what *he* believed, was a patriot. Men knew that other men, of every persuasion, were interested in the welfare, safety, and development of the country.

It is no exaggeration to say that the age of the Confederation was an era of good feeling. Those of one political persuasion did not doubt the high-minded motives of their opponents. Everyone took it for granted that his foes as well as his friends wanted to advance the interests of the United States. Few stooped to the level of personal attacks, and everyone assumed that every American was a gentleman.

"We are one, an united people," the Pennsylvania *Gazette* said in November, 1786. Virtually everyone in the country accepted that simple statement at face value. Only the ignorant and the bigoted would have argued the matter.

Certainly no American willingly would have accepted reunion with Great Britain. Every citizen, be he a national- or a state-government advocate, prized the country's independence. In fact, the Massachusetts *Centinel*, replying to the Pennsylvania *Gazette*, said in December, 1786, that tens of thousands of Americans who had not taken up arms during the Revolution would rush to the nation's defense if the British tried to recapture the country by force of arms.

Only on the frontier was the situation seemingly different. In the Kentucky district of Virginia and the Franklin district of North Carolina, the wilderness men flirted with Spain. They accepted her gold, listened to her promises, knowing they could not be kept, and occasionally muttered that they were interested in secession. But they had no intention of leaving the United States and joining forces with Spain. Why, then, did they pretend?

General John Sevier, the undisputed leader of Franklin, broke away from North Carolina and formed his own state. Sevier and his associates, men like William

Cocke, the Reverend Samuel Houston, and Arthur Campbell, were dedicated patriots who had served their country with great distinction during the Revolution. Sevier, in fact, was a great national hero, the victor in the Battle of King's Mountain (1780) in the North Carolina Campaign, the most important military engagement with the Redcoats in the West.

All these men, it must be emphasized, later served the United States—Tennessee, Virginia, and other states—with lifelong devotion. Sevier, the pioneer statesman-soldier, was the idol of the West. A superb Indian fighter, he is believed to have fought in more than eighty campaigns against tribes that tried to make life on the frontier untenable for the settlers. In all, Sevier spent about sixteen years as Governor of Franklin and of its successor, Tennessee, the latter for six terms. He also spent four terms in the United States House of Representatives.

Colonel Arthur Campbell, who also fought with great honor at King's Mountain, was prominent in the development of both Tennessee and Kentucky. Campbell County in the latter state is named in his honor.

The reputation of the remarkable William Cocke in the eighteenth century was as great as that of Patrick Henry and Thomas Jefferson. Americans everywhere revered this veteran of the Revolution, and he was believed by many to be the greatest legislator of his age. The first United States Senator from Tennessee, he volunteered for service as a private in the War of 1812, even though well into his sixties. A restless frontier dweller who frequently moved to new pioneer lands, he served in the legislatures of Virginia, North Carolina, Tennessee, Mississippi, and two territorial assemblies.

The Reverend Samuel Houston never became as famous as his grandnephew of the same name, who served as Governor of Tennessee and of Texas, and was President of the Republic of Texas before guiding her into the Union. But the elder Samuel Houston, who was Franklin's first clergyman before moving back to his native Virginia, was loved by thousands of his fellow Americans. A veteran of the Revolution, he was ordained as a Presbyterian minister in 1782, and served without interruption until his death in 1839. He also was a trustee of Washington College for many years.

Judge David Campbell, a Revolutionary War veteran, was Chief Justice of Franklin. He was a justice of the Tennessee Superior Court from the time the state was admitted to the Union in 1796 until his death in 1811.

General David Kennedy, a war veteran and noted Indian fighter, was another of Franklin's prominent citizens. He developed an abiding interest in education, and was personally responsible for the erection of many schools in Tennessee. He also served as a trustee of Greeneville and Washington Colleges.

Colonel Stockley Donelson was Franklin's surveyor, and he showed little interest in politics. Eventually he became one of Tennessee's largest landowners; at one time his estates were estimated at about half a million acres. He was the brother-in-law of President Andrew Jackson.

It is inconceivable that these leaders of Franklin, along with a score of others whose records are equally patriotic, could have been traitors to the United States.

Nevertheless they *did* flirt with Spain. And there was alarm in the older parts of the United States, in 1788 and 1789, that Franklin might secede and form an independent nation allied with Spain.

Actually, Sevier and his associates were playing a very clever and devious game. North Carolina steadily and stubbornly refused to give up its own claims to the territory known as Franklin. When the leaders of Franklin formed their own state, North Carolina refused to recognize it.

Seeking the support of Benjamin Franklin, after whom they had named their state, Governor John Sevier and his associates applied to the Continental Congress for admission to the Union. William Cocke, one of the most talented orators of his time, went to Philadelphia as Franklin's delegate to plead for the support of his state.

The established states with no territorial claims of their own in the West were sympathetic to Franklin's cause. Pennsylvania was the first to pledge its unqualified support. New York, Massachusetts, and New Jersey soon followed Pennsylvania's example. With the help of such powerful friends, the cause of Franklin appeared bright.

But North Carolina worked furiously to prevent the new state's admission to the Union. It was closely supported by Virginia, who was afraid to lose its own Kentucky district under similar circumstances. The fight that followed was one of the most violent in the brief history of the Confederation.

The approval of nine states was needed for Franklin to win. Only eight states supported the bid, and Cocke went home, bitterly disappointed.

Franklin's friends in Congress advised the state to try

again. It did, repeatedly, but without success. It was obvious that something was needed to change the minds of the delegates representing one of the five states blocking the admission. Sevier and his associates decided to try bold tactics. They opened their flirtation with Spain, pretending they were seriously considering secession. Their private correspondence indicates, however, that they were merely bluffing. Even the Spaniards themselves were fooled for only a short time, and thereafter suspected the truth.

Circumstances made it unnecessary for Franklin to carry out its threat or back down by admitting it didn't mean to secede. In 1789, when the Constitution was adopted, the situation changed drastically. The national government became stronger, and a handful of states with claims to Western lands could no longer prevent the admission of new states.

Franklin was reorganized, and began to work toward statehood as Tennessee. Vermont and Kentucky preceded it into the Union, but its own story had a happy ending when Tennessee was admitted as soon as it applied.

Certainly the case of Franklin emphasizes the weakness of the United States under the Confederation. If men were not seriously worried, and most were not, it was because the nation was enjoying both freedom and great prosperity, neither of which she had ever experienced. Such newspapers as the Pennsylvania *Gazette* and the Massachusetts *Centinel,* along with several dozen smaller, less influential organs, consistently supported the demands for a revised governmental system.

But they refused to depict the lot of Americans as

desperate, or even unhappy. The *Centinel* showed little sympathy for the small minority who were afraid the country would collapse. A *Centinel* editorial in August, 1787, said:

> The complaints of the decay of trade are without foundation. It should rather be said there is a decay of a few traders. We need less than we have. A few merchants are sufficient to import and sell all the goods America requires. Let those of them who complain of hard times betake themselves to the cultivation of the earth, or to the establishment of some useful manufacture. Until ninety-nine out of an hundred of the citizens of America are farmers, artificers or manufacturers, we can never be completely happy. But we are becoming more so, just as we are growing richer, and our citizens will not heed the plaintive cries of those who would bury America.

By 1787, men in every walk of life came to realize that in spite of her growth and prosperity the United States was no paradise. The weakness of the Confederation had become apparent, and the country was fortunate that no major dangers had threatened her survival. Alexander Hamilton was convinced that the states would find it impossible to band together effectively in the event a new war broke out with a major European power. It was urgent, he said, that the national government be strengthened as soon as possible.

Patrick Henry, the ardent advocate of the rights of the states, did not agree. A strong national government, he contended, would make it possible for a tyrant to seize control. "A man such as this," he wrote to Jefferson in Paris, "could make himself king of America. And no one could stay his hand. When I think of the peril that may engulf us if the states lose their powers of veto, I dare not sleep at night for fear that my nightmares may choke the breath from my body and destroy my mind."

Henry's reply to Hamilton was simple. The states had found it possible to work together in 1775 and 1776. If external danger threatened, they would be able to stand together again.

Hamilton retorted that the great Virginian was explaining things in terms that were too simple. The population had increased so much and the United States had expanded so far across the mountains that no group of states, acting as individual units, could function effectively in time of war. Only a single government with power over all the states could manage.

Similarly, Hamilton declared, the states bickered so much that they would be unable to agree on a course of action in the event of economic disaster. If the present economic boom came to an end, the states would not be able to pass uniform laws to improve the situation. No two states had similar laws now, and it was too much to expect that they would change. Merchants, farmers, and manufacturers everywhere were demanding uniform laws. Chaos would result if Massachusetts, Maryland, and South Carolina did not work together toward the same ends.

The pressures for a new type of government were growing, and would become irresistible. The Constitutional Convention of 1787 was a direct outgrowth of those pressures.

IX. The End of an Era—1789

The thirteen states, James Madison wryly observed early in 1787, were behaving like naughty children who were no longer under the supervision of their parents. In theory, most of the thirteen colonies had exercised self-government in their domestic affairs. In practice, however, Great Britain had kept a tight hold on the reins all through the years before the Revolution. Royal governors, Parliament, and the Colonial Office in London had found ways to veto and otherwise disapprove of new ideas and unorthodox measures.

The winning of the war had been the first consideration of the new states. Until 1781, virtually no one had dared look ahead to the building of an expanding nation that was at peace with the world. The Battle of Yorktown caused a major change in the thinking of all Americans, and nowhere was this more evident than in its own interests, often at the expense of its neighbors. Few men were accustomed to thinking of the United States as a whole, and few did.

"We are thirteen stallions, each galloping in a different direction," Benjamin Franklin said about a year after his return home from Europe. "I wonder that we have not torn apart the coach of state."

Every American wanted his share of the new good life. The Confederation had no power to grant the demands of individuals and groups, so the states were besieged with requests for help of all kinds.

The first organized pressure group in the country was the Society of Cincinnati, a club of war veterans formed by Major General Henry Knox and a number of his friends. Politically ambitious ex-officers saw an opportunity to exercise influence through the Society, and were active in forming chapters everywhere. By 1783, the Society, still growing, could be found in every state, in every frontier district.

Most of the veterans had not been paid their full wages for military service, and wanted what was owed them. They also wanted pensions for every man, special grants to those who had been wounded, and, above all, free land on the frontier.

The Continental Congress was swamped with demands by many chapters and branches of the Society of Cincinnati. But the war veterans were realists, and knew that Congress had no funds of its own to hand out to them, no power to give away land that belonged to the states. So, naturally, even greater pressure was applied to the state legislatures, where many prominent former soldiers were already serving.

The situation of each state determined its attitude toward the veterans. Connecticut, which had suffered

little war damage, was wealthy and growing wealthier.
So her legislature could afford to be generous. Every
veteran of the Connecticut militia was awarded a pen-
sion and a certificate—which later proved worthless—en-
titling the holder to claim free land in the territory
Connecticut was claiming in the Ohio Valley.

The South Carolina veteran enjoyed no such benefits
in the years immediately following the war. Much of the
state had been reduced to ruins by the armies of both
sides during years of hard fighting. Farms had been
burned and houses destroyed. Cotton and indigo, the
chief crops, were not yet showing a profit. Charleston,
which the Redcoats did not evacuate until 1782, needed
time to recover its place as a major seaport.

So, until 1785, the South Carolina legislature could
do no more than make promises to her veterans, and the
former soldiers had to wait a long time for both cash
and land. Naturally they were bitter, and clamored for
benefits like those enjoyed by their comrades-in-arms
from Connecticut.

General Washington's Continentals, who had formed
the regular army backbone of the American armed forces,
were in the most unfortunate position of all. Since they
had not served the individual states, they could make
no claims on the state governments. Their employer had
been the weak Continental Congress, and they turned to
it for assistance.

But the Confederation government, it must be remembered, had no authority to raise money in its own right.
It depended completely on the governments of the thirteen states for its funds. The state legislatures, trying to

fulfill direct demands from people of all classes, refused to give more than token sums to the Confederation.

So the Continental veterans, who had done more than any other group to win the war, enjoyed none of the benefits of victory. Instead they watched money and lands being handed to the inferior state militia, whom they long had despised as inefficient bumblers. It is not surprising that they were bitter.

They knew they could hope for help only from a stronger national government. So, of course, they were among the first to call for a government of all Americans, a government that could raise revenues on its own authority and could dispense funds without the specific approval of the individual states.

Many men, like Patrick Henry, who were afraid a tyrant might rise to take power, did not trust the military. Throughout history dictators had used armies to help them seize and hold the reins of government. Someone ruthless and unprincipled might use the Society of Cincinnati for the same purpose. Therefore, just as the Continental veterans fervently wanted a stronger national government, the advocates of decentralized power were opposed to a reorganization.

Others were equally insistent in demanding help from the government, among them merchants, manufacturers, and farmers. Since each state passed its own import and export laws, the merchants and manufacturers appealed to the thirteen legislatures for laws that would make it easier for them to make their products, sell them abroad, and buy other goods that the American people wanted.

The legislatures tried, to the best of their ability, to meet the demands of each state's citizens. Since these needs varied, the laws varied, too. The result was a crazy quilt that hampered trade. A Boston shipowner, for example, was not subject only to the laws of Massachusetts. If his vessel called at New York and Philadelphia, Baltimore and Charleston, as it might have to do in order to make a profitable voyage, he was compelled also to obey the laws of New York, Pennsylvania, Maryland, and South Carolina.

Massachusetts, which wanted to encourage the building of small merchant ships, levied an insignificant tax of only three dollars on ships up to one thousand tons entering Boston Harbor. All vessels of more than one thousand tons were required to pay a considerable port tax of twenty-five dollars. So the first ships that John Hancock built after the war were constructed to take advantage of this law. Each was of nine hundred tons.

New York, desperate for funds after the war, levied a thirty-dollar port tax on every ship of more than seven hundred tons. Pennsylvania, on behalf of Philadelphia, was almost as greedy. And Hancock naturally complained that he could not earn a profitable living if his ships put into ports other than Boston. Not only was he required to pay a different state tax in every port, but most of those taxes were exorbitantly high. He could do far better, he said, by ordering his captains to stay away from American ports other than Boston, and confine their calls to European and West Indian ports.

In the states of the North, where commerce and manufacturing were expanding rapidly, the merchants and manufacturers who were hampered by conflicting state laws were among the most ardent supporters of a strengthened national government. In the South, however, a different situation existed. There the plantations and farms were growing rapidly. But the laws of other states made it difficult and expensive for them to send their products across state lines.

In 1786, for example, Henry Rutledge, a prominent plantation owner, complained bitterly in the South Carolina legislature about the restrictions imposed on cotton by other states. It was cheaper, he said, to send his cotton to England than to Connecticut and New York. Yet there was a great demand for South Carolina cotton in both of these Northern states. Shortsighted laws passed by their legislatures lowered the profits of the South Carolina planter and denied the New York and Connecticut factory owners the cotton they needed to keep their plants in operation.

Inevitably, an alliance was formed between the merchants and manufacturers of the North on one hand and the farmers of the South on the other. All clamored together for a strengthened national government. Their opponents claimed that only the rich would benefit, and that it was in the interests of the ordinary citizen to surrender no states' rights to a national government.

It is true that the wealthy banded together, but their foes exaggerated the situation. It became evident, particularly in the larger cities and increasingly industrialized towns of the United States, that a stronger national government would be a great help also to the artisan.

Nails were being made in small factories, for example,

as was everything else from gloves, stockings, and shoes
to spinning-wheel irons. All these items—hundreds of different consumer goods—were being turned out by skilled
craftsmen. But since no national law existed to regulate
the importation of foreign goods, it was possible for English nailmakers to send kegs of nails by the thousands
into the United States. This threatened ruin for the American nailmakers.

Pennsylvania tried to protect its local manufacturers
and artisans by passing a law that established a stiff import tax on imported nails. But neighboring Delaware had
no such law. So it was a simple matter for British exporters
to send their nails to Delaware. Local merchants there
gave in to the temptation of smuggling them across the
Pennsylvania state line. And, since these merchants made
a profit, they ignored the bitter complaints of Pennsylvania nailmakers and the Pennsylvania legislature.

The attempts of British manufacturers and exporters
to recapture the American markets they had controlled
before the war caused complications in many fields. The
laws regulating imports and import taxes were different
in every state. The smuggling of many items other than
nails was common, too. Skilled artisans, who were known
in the eighteenth and early nineteenth centuries as
"mechanics," feared the loss of their jobs and became
alarmed.

Small local newspapers in the increasingly industrial
states were filled with letters that stressed one theme.
American artisans had to be protected, the writers declared, or the nation would become bankrupt within a
decade.

The shoemakers of Philadelphia were the first to suffer. After enjoying an ever increasing volume of business in the years immediately after the end of the war, they suddenly found, in 1786, that there was no more demand for their product. Shoes were being imported inexpensively from England. British merchants, hoping to change the buying habits of Americans, were selling their shoes for almost ridiculously low prices.

The Philadelphia shoemakers banded together. They announced they would not buy, sell, or mend imported shoes. The shoemakers of Boston greeted this declaration with a statement of their own. Their colleagues, they said, had set a noble example for all citizens. The movement spread, and by the middle of 1786, thousands of artisans in scores of towns had taken an oath to buy no English-made shoes.

The British promptly retaliated by cutting off their importation of American cedar, even though the wood was badly needed by cabinetmakers in London and other cities. American merchants in the export-import business understood the significance of what was taking place. American trade, on which the future prosperity of the nation depended, was in jeopardy.

The sensible solution of the problem seemed obvious to the merchants. American manufacturers and artisans needed protection, but it was necessary, at the same time, to encourage foreign trade. These twin objectives could be achieved only by the passage of carefully devised laws. The regulation of trade would require supervision, which meant that the laws probably would have

to be changed every year or two, depending on the flow
of imports and exports.

The merchants, supported by the artisans, bombarded
the state legislatures with pleas and demands for uniform laws governing commerce. Each legislature, jealous
of its rights, passed bills that afforded protection only
for the manufacturers and artisans of its own state. An
already muddled situation became worse.

By the beginning of 1787, merchants were loudly demanding that the Continental Congress be given full
control of both international and interstate trade. The
legislatures paid virtually no attention to the clamor, and
nothing was done.

Then, in February, 1787, the "mechanics" of Boston
lost their patience and tempers. A group of several hundred marched on the State House, and when legislators
came out after a day's business session, they were greeted
with a barrage of jeers. Then someone pulled a cobble-
stone from the street, and a riot broke out. The local
constabulary, sympathizing with the rioters, refused to
interfere.

A few days later a crowd of about one thousand New
York artisans, sailors, and other workingmen marched
through the streets of the city, demanding the formation
of a national government that would preserve their prosperity. Philadelphia averted a similar scene only by
calling out the constabulary in advance, so the city's
artisans stayed at home.

The overall problem of strengthening the national government had become general, and was recognized by

men of every class. "We are facing a dilemma that is both political and economic in nature," James Madison said. "How can we preserve our liberties, including our independence as a nation, if we become permanently bankrupt?"

Complications within the state legislatures increased the confusion. Almost everywhere there was growing rivalry between the seacoast towns and the hinterlands. Men in the back country were claiming, with some justification, that population centers were moving inland. Therefore they wanted state capitals transferred closer to their own homes and businesses. Naturally the seacoast communities resisted. The squabble so thoroughly occupied many of the legislatures that the larger problems of forming a stronger national government were ignored or given only slight attention.

South Carolina had been dominated by Charleston since its earliest days. But, in the years immediately following the war, the farmers and planters of the interior gained enough prominence to demand that the capital be moved. In 1786, a site was chosen in the center of the state, and the first buildings were erected in Columbia, which actually became the capital three years later.

North Carolina was less fortunate. The state saw so much fighting during the war that the legislature moved frequently, and no one was satisfied with the prewar capital, New Bern. No less than eleven different sites were proposed in the postwar years, each with its champions. The argument was so bitter that the site of the permanent capital, Raleigh, was not selected until 1792, three years after the Constitution went into effect.

Georgia was forced to evacuate its old capital, Savannah, when the British occupied the town during the war. The legislature met in Augusta, and after the war shifted back and forth several times between that town and Savannah. In 1786, the legislature shifted to Augusta for the last time, but Savannah refused for several years to recognize the new, permanent capital.

Virginia's squabble was conducted on a dignified basis befitting the oldest and most patrician of states. The capital was moved to Richmond, a new town, in 1779. The older sections of the state tried to return the government to Williamsburg after the war, but their efforts were defeated by the residents of newly settled counties.

In New Hampshire, the men of the West won a sharp battle. The partisans of Portsmouth, the old capital, refused to yield, but the frontiersmen insisted on moving to the center of the state. In 1782, the legislature convened in Concord, eventually the permanent capital, and refused to return to Portsmouth.

Albany became the capital of New York in 1776, when New York Town was occupied by the Redcoats. Residents of the rapidly growing seaport expected to become the center of state government again at the end of the war. But the legislature, supported by the state's farmers, stubbornly refused to move.

Back-country Pennsylvanians were jealous of Philadelphia's prominence, and made repeated efforts to remove the capital inland. In 1785, the state officially accepted land offered by John Harris, the founder of Harrisburg, but Philadelphia refused to yield, and not until 1812 was the capital moved to Harrisburg, after a brief sojourn in Lancaster.

Boston so thoroughly dominated Massachusetts that efforts to move the capital inland were totally unsuccessful. Residents of the interior were very bitter, however, and relations between the seacoast and the hinterland remained strained for many years because of the dispute.

We know of the explosive demand for statehood in the West. But the influence of the West on the formation of a new national government can be seen in perspective only in relation to similar uprisings elsewhere. Residents of Vermont knew they would not be granted the right to form their own state while the Confederation was hobbled by the rule demanding the approval of nine old states. New Hampshire, the Vermonters knew, would not give up its frontier lands unless forced to do so.

Realistic frontiersmen in growing, booming Kentucky were ready for statehood by 1786 or 1787. Virginia refused to entertain the possibility, however, and Kentuckians became ardent advocates of a new national government. So did the men of Franklin, some of whom actually fought pitched battles with residents of their mother state, North Carolina.

The urban dwellers of the East sympathized with the men of the West. Only a few years had passed since the entire country had won its freedom, and the people in the cities and towns of the seaboard vividly remembered how it had felt to be under the domination of outsiders. There was a strong surge of public opinion in favor of the Westerners. They had as much right as any other Americans to govern themselves, the Easterners felt. This attitude caused an erosion in the official positions of New Hampshire, Virginia, and North Carolina, even though those who refused to relinquish the frontier lands still held power.

This sympathy for the frontiersman was felt very strongly in the major population centers. For example, when William Cocke of Franklin went to Philadelphia to present his state's case to the Continental Congress, crowds followed him every day, cheering him. And huge throngs gathered outside his rooming house to serenade him with "The Liberty Tree" and other popular wartime songs that extolled the rights of Americans to be free.

Only a few Western counties sent representatives to the state legislatures of New Hampshire, Virginia, and North Carolina. These men had only a minor voice and little influence in the affairs of the mother states. So, for all practical purposes, the West was not represented, either directly or indirectly, in the Continental Congress.

But the frontiersman, making a new life for himself and his family in the wilderness, had kindled the imagination and captured the sympathy of the rest of the country. The Westerner was seen as a man who was already fighting against great odds, and his gallantry won him both the friendship and the firm support of thousands. The stay-at-homes respected him, admired him, and added their voices to the demands that a stronger national government be formed and new states created in the West.

Another factor that was leading the states toward the substitution of a stronger central government for the Confederation was a need of their own that became stronger every year. Necessity forced the individual states to work together, but they found it very hard to settle their disputes amicably. A greater authority was required to impose a settlement of interstate arguments.

New York and Massachusetts, for example, discovered in 1783 that they were claiming the same land on the border that separated them. They appealed to the Continental Congress for help, and the judiciary committee appointed a panel of three judges to hear the case. The judges, not wanting to be caught in the middle, refused to serve. So the two states had to appoint a joint commission of their own. The commissioners wrangled and debated for the better part of four years, and the boundary wasn't settled until 1787, at considerable cost to both New York and Massachusetts.

Maryland and Virginia both were interested in the use of the Potomac River and the opening of its waters to navigation. A long argument riddled the legislatures of both states before it was finally agreed that Virginia would pay five dollars for every three spent by Maryland in developing the river. Meanwhile the actual work of broadening and deepening the Potomac had to wait.

Pennsylvania and Delaware became embroiled in a bitter argument, in 1781, regarding the use of the Delaware River, which was essential to the commerce of both states. Necessity forced the joint commission appointed to settle the dispute to remain in session, but a year passed before an agreement satisfactory to both sides was reached. Then the Delaware and Pennsylvania legislatures spent another year quibbling and exchanging accusations, and the agreement was not ratified until late in 1783.

"The Delaware River question," Robert Morris said, "should have been submitted to the Confederation Congress for arbitration. The Congress should have been empowered to make a final decision binding on both states. That which took two years could have been resolved in two months, at a saving of many millions of dollars to the shippers and merchants of these states. Disagreements of this sort, which defy the senses of philosophically inclined men, make imperative the formation of a government that can make its will felt upon the recalcitrant states of this imperfect Union."

The failure of the Confederation was only relative, however. This, above all, must be remembered about the period prior to the adoption of the Constitution. Americans were conducting their first experiment in self-government, and their achievements were considerable.

The Continental Congress provided a forum for the exchange of opinions on a national scale. Men from New England learned what the South thought on a given subject. The South discovered the reasons for New England's attitudes. When disputes arose, it was common for both sides to seek compromises. Democracy, as James Madison observed, was a form of government that could succeed only through compromise.

The Continental Congress formed the core of a central government. Experts—in foreign affairs and finance, the development of roads and waterways, the postal service, and on relations with the Indians—served for years during the Confederation. These men became accustomed to thinking in national rather than regional or state terms.

Most of them continued to work for the government after the Constitution had been adopted. The day-to-day administration of the government depended exclusively on their efforts. A half century later, President James K. Polk observed that these selfless, hard-working men were the original civil service. They served at small salaries, without glory or even recognition, because they loved their country and were determined that she should succeed.

These men spent a generation in the government, and the Administrations of the first Presidents completely depended on them. It is no exaggeration to say that these loyal citizens were the first American nationalists, the first, perhaps, to recognize the need for a stronger central government.

One of the greatest accomplishments of the Confederation era was the creation of the national domain, that is, large areas of land owned by the United States government on behalf of all the people. The problems in setting up the national domain were as complex as they were enormous. This was due in part to the selfishness of the states, in part to the efforts of land speculators to keep these lands in private hands.

For all practical purposes, the national domain came into being in 1784, when the Continental Congress accepted Virginia's cession of the huge Northwest Territory.

In handing this vast tract to the national government, Virginia wasn't motivated by generosity or patriotism. Kentucky, which it kept, was all it could comfortably administer, all her taxpayers could afford to keep. The Confederation was made a gift of the vast territory because Virginia didn't know what else to do with these millions of acres.

Eventually other states ceded land to the Confederation, too, and the basis was laid for a policy fundamental to the ultimate successful expansion of the United States across the North American continent. Territories were administered by the national government until they applied for statehood and were admitted to the Union as states. Land in the territories was available to any man in lots of reasonable size, usually one hundred and sixty acres. Depending on the demand, a man either received his claim free of charge or paid a nominal sum for it.

Some portions of the land, however, were kept by the Confederation. This land subsequently was used for schools, for public waterways, or, later, made into land preserves. The nation's many land-grant schools owe their existence to this far-sighted policy, as does the beginning of the program of conserving the nation's natural resources for the use of all.

When the members of the Constitutional Convention met in Philadelphia, in May, 1787, and drew up the remarkable document that has been the basis of the United States' form of government for the better part of two hundred years, they were accused by the advocates of states' rights of abandoning the Confederation. Madison, who, more than any other man, perhaps, was responsible for drawing up the Constitution, had a reply ready for them.

"We do not abandon the Confederation," he said, "any more than loving parents abandon a child found wanting. We, the American people, are the parents of the Confederation. Through the new Constitution we are making it more self-reliant, stronger, better able to cope with the problems and dangers which we, as a free and independent people living in a free and independent land, must face."

On June 21, 1788, New Hampshire, the ninth state to do so, ratified the new Constitution, and the new Federal government of the United States was born. But time was needed to establish the machinery of government, and the Constitution did not become effective until March 4, 1789. On that date, the Confederation ceased to exist. An era came to an end, but in a larger sense the Confederation did not die. Instead it was incorporated in the new, better form of government, and became a permanent part of the heritage of the American people.

Appendix

Articles of Confederation
and Perpetual Union

To all to whom these Presents shall come, we the undersigned Delegates of the States affixed to our Names send greeting. Whereas the Delegates of the United States of America in Congress assembled did on the fifteenth day of November in the Year of our Lord One Thousand Seven Hundred and Seventy seven, and in the Second Year of the Independence of America agree to certain articles of Confederation and perpetual Union between the States of Newhampshire, Massachusetts-bay, Rhode-island and Providence Plantations, Connecticut, New York, New Jersey, Pennsylvania, Delaware, Maryland, Virginia, North-Carolina, South-Carolina and Georgia in the Words following, viz. "Articles of Confederation and perpetual Union between the states of Newhampshire, Massachusetts-bay, Rhodeisland and Providence

Plantations, Connecticut, New-York, New-Jersey, Pennsylvania, Delaware, Maryland, Virginia, North-Carolina, South-Carolina, and Georgia."

Art. I. The Stile of this confederacy shall be "The United States of America."

Art. II. Each state retains its sovereignty, freedom and independence, and every Power, Jurisdiction and right, which is not by this confederation expressly delegated to the United States, in Congress assembled.

Art. III. The said states hereby severally enter into a firm league of friendship with each other, for their common defence, the security of their Liberties, and their mutual and general welfare, binding themselves to assist each other, against all force offered to, or attacks made upon them, or any of them, on account of religion, sovereignty, trade, or any other pretence whatever.

Art. IV. The better to secure and perpetuate mutual friendship and intercourse among the people of the different states in this union, the free inhabitants of each of these states, paupers, vagabonds and fugitives from Justice excepted, shall be entitled to all privileges and immunities of free citizens in the several states; and the people of each state shall have free ingress and regress to and from any other state, and shall enjoy therein all the privileges of trade and commerce, subject to the same duties, impositions and restrictions as the inhabitants thereof respectively, provided that such restriction shall not extend so far as to prevent the removal of property imported into any state, to any other state of which the Owner is an inhabitant; provided also that no imposition, duties or restriction shall be laid by any state, on the property of the united states, or either of them.

If any Person guilty of, or charged with treason, felony, or other high misdemeanor in any state, shall flee
from Justice, and be found in any of the united states, he
shall upon demand of the Governor or executive power,
of the state from which he fled, be delivered up and
removed to the state having jurisdiction of his offence.

Full faith and credit shall be given in each of these
states to the records, acts and judicial proceedings of
the courts and magistrates of every other state.

Art. V. For the more convenient management of the
general interests of the united states, delegates shall be
annually appointed in such manner as the legislature of
each state shall direct, to meet in Congress on the first
Monday in November, in every year, with a power reserved to each state, to recal its delegates, or any of
them, at any time within the year, and to send others
in their stead, for the remainder of the Year.

No state shall be represented in Congress by less than
two, nor by more than seven Members; and no person
shall be capable of being a delegate for more than three
years in any term of six years; nor shall any person,
being a delegate, be capable of holding any office under
the united states, for which he, or another for his benefit
receives any salary, fees or emolument of any kind.

Each state shall maintain its own delegates in a meeting of the states, and while they act as members of the
committee of the states.

In determining questions in the united states, in Congress assembled, each state shall have one vote.

Freedom of speech and debate in Congress shall not
be impeached or questioned in any Court, or place out
of Congress, and the members of congress shall be pro-

tected in their persons from arrests and imprisonments, during the time of their going to and from, and attendance on congress, except for treason, felony, or breach of the peace.

Art. VI. No state without the Consent of the united states in congress assembled, shall send any embassy to, or receive any embassy from, or enter into any conference, agreement, or alliance or treaty with any King, prince or state; nor shall any person holding any office of profit or trust under the united states, or any of them, accept of any present, emolument, office or title of any kind whatever from any king, prince or foreign state; nor shall the united states in congress assembled, or any of them, grant any title of nobility.

No two or more states shall enter into any treaty, confederation or alliance whatever between them, without the consent of the united states in congress assembled, specifying accurately the purposes for which the same is to be entered into, and how long it shall continue.

No state shall lay any imposts or duties, which may interfere with any stipulations in treaties, entered into by the united states in congress assembled, with any king, prince or state, in pursuance of any treaties already proposed by congress, to the courts of France and Spain.

No vessels of war shall be kept up in time of peace by any state, except such number only, as shall be deemed necessary by the united states in congress assembled, for the defence of such state, or its trade; nor shall any body of forces be kept up by any state, in time of peace, except such number only, as in the judgment of the united states, in congress assembled, shall be deemed requisite to garrison the forts necessary for the defence of such state; but every state shall always keep up a well regulated and disciplined militia, sufficiently armed and accoutred, and shall provide and constantly have ready for use, in public stores, a due number of field pieces and tents, and a proper quantity of arms, ammunition and camp equipage.

No state shall engage in any war without the consent of the united states in congress assembled, unless such state be actually invaded by enemies, or shall have received certain advice of a resolution being formed by some nation of Indians to invade such state, and the danger is so imminent as not to admit of a delay, till the united states in congress assembled can be consulted: nor shall any state grant commissions to any ships or vessels of war, nor letters of marque or reprisal, except it be after a declaration of war by the united states in congress assembled, and then only against the kingdom or state and the subjects thereof, against which war has been so declared, and under such regulations as shall be established by the united states in congress assembled, unless such state be infested by pirates, in which case vessels of war may be fitted out for that occasion, and kept so long as the danger shall continue, or until the united states in congress assembled shall determine otherwise.

Art. VII. When land-forces are raised by any state for the common defence, all officers of or under the rank of colonel, shall be appointed by the legislature of each state respectively by whom such forces shall be raised, or in such manner as such state shall direct, and all vacancies shall be filled up by the state which first made the appointment.

Art. VIII. All charges of war, and all other expences that shall be incurred for the common defence or general welfare, and allowed by the united states in congress assembled, shall be defrayed out of a common treasury, which shall be supplied by the several states, in proportion to the value of all land within each state, granted to or surveyed for any Person, as such land and the buildings and improvements thereon shall be estimated according to such mode as the united states in congress assembled, shall from time to time direct and appoint. The taxes for paying that proportion shall be laid and levied by the authority and direction of the legislatures of the several states within the time agreed upon by the united states in congress assembled.

Art. IX. The united states in congress assembled, shall have the sole and exclusive right and power of determining on peace and war, except in the cases mentioned in the sixth article—of sending and receiving ambassadors—entering into treaties and alliances, provided that no treaty of commerce shall be made whereby the legislative power of the respective states shall be restrained from imposing such imposts and duties on foreigners, as their own people are subjected to, or from prohibiting the exportation or importation of any species of goods or commodities whatsoever—of establishing rules for deciding in all cases, what captures on land or water shall be legal, and in what manner prizes taken by land or naval forces in the service of the united states shall be divided or appropriated—of granting letters of marque and reprisal in times of peace—appointing courts for the trial of piracies and felonies committed on the high seas and establishing courts for receiving and determining finally appeals in all cases of captures, provided that no member of congress shall be appointed a judge of any of the said courts.

The united states in congress assembled shall also be the last resort on appeal in all disputes and differences now subsisting or that hereafter may arise between two or more states concerning boundary, jurisdiction or any other cause whatever; which authority shall always be exercised in the manner following. Whenever the legislative or executive authority or lawful agent of any state in controversy with another shall present a petition to congress, stating the matter in question and praying for a hearing, notice thereof shall be given by order of congress to the legislative or executive authority of the other state in controversy, and a day assigned for the appearance of the parties by their lawful agents, who shall then be directed to appoint by joint consent, commissioners or judges to constitute a court for hearing and determining the matter in question: but if they cannot agree, congress shall name three persons out of each of the united states, and from the list of such persons each party shall alternately strike out one, the petitioners beginning, until the number shall be reduced to thirteen; and from that number not less than seven, nor more than nine names as congress shall direct, shall in the presence of congress be drawn out by lot, and the persons whose names shall be so drawn or any five of them, shall be commissioners or judges, to hear and finally determine the controversy, so always as a major part of the judges who shall hear the cause shall agree in the determination: and if either party shall neglect to attend at the day appointed, without shewing reasons, which congress shall judge sufficient, or being present shall refuse to strike, the congress shall proceed to nominate three persons out of each state, and the secretary of congress shall strike in behalf of such party absent or refusing; and the judgment and sentence of the court to be appointed, in the manner before prescribed, shall be final and conclusive; and if any of the parties shall refuse to submit to the authority of such court, or to appear to defend their claim, or cause, the court shall nevertheless proceed to pronounce sentence, or judgment, which shall in like manner be final and decisive, the judgment or sentence and other proceedings being in either case transmitted to congress, and lodged among the acts of congress for the security of the parties concerned: provided that every commissioner, before he sits in judgment, shall take an oath to be administered by one of the judges of the supreme or superior court of the state, where the cause shall be tried, "well and truly to hear and determine the matter in question, according to the best of his judgment, without favour, affection or hope of reward:" provided also that no state shall be deprived of territory for the benefit of the united states.

All controversies concerning the private right of soil claimed under different grants of two or more states, whose jurisdictions as they may respect such lands, and the states which passed such grants are adjusted, the said grants or either of them being at the same time

claimed to have originated antecedent to such settlement of jurisdiction, shall on the petition of either party
to the congress of the united states, be finally determined
as near as may be in the same manner as is before prescribed for deciding disputes respecting territorial jurisdiction between different states.

The united states in congress assembled shall also have
the sole and exclusive right and power of regulating the
alloy and value of coin struck by their own authority,
or by that of the respective states—fixing the standard of
weights and measures throughout the united states—regulating the trade and managing all affairs with the Indians, not members of any of the states, provided that
the legislative right of any state within its own limits
be not infringed or violated—establishing and regulating
post-offices from one state to another, throughout all the
united states, and exacting such postage on the papers
passing thro' the same as may be requisite to defray the
expences of the said office—appointing all officers of the
land forces, in the service of the united states, excepting
regimental officers—appointing all the officers of the naval
forces, and commissioning all officers whatever in the
service of the united states—making rules for the government and regulation of the said land and naval forces,
and directing their operations.

The united states in congress assembled shall have
authority to appoint a committee, to sit in the recess of
congress, to be denominated "A Committee of the States,"
and to consist of one delegate from each state; and to
appoint such other committees and civil officers as may
be necessary for managing the general affairs of the

united states under their direction—to appoint one of
their number to preside, provided that no person be allowed to serve in the office of president more than one
year in any term of three years; to ascertain the necessary
sums of Money to be raised for the service of the united
states, and to appropriate and apply the same for de-
fraying the public expences—to borrow money, or emit
bills on the credit of the united states, transmitting every
half year to the respective states an account of the sums
of money so borrowed or emitted—to build and equip a
navy—to agree upon the number of land forces, and to
make requisitions from each state for its quota, in proportion to the number of white inhabitants in such state;
which requisition shall be binding, and thereupon the
legislature of each state shall appoint the regimental officers, raise the men and cloath, arm and equip them in
a soldier like manner, at the expence of the united states,
and the officers and men so cloathed, armed and
equipped shall march to the place appointed, and within
the time agreed on by the united states in congress assembled: But if the united states in congress assembled
shall, on consideration of circumstances judge proper that
any state should not raise men, or should raise a smaller
number than its quota, and that any other state should
raise a greater number of men than the quota thereof,
such extra number shall be raised, officered, cloathed,
armed and equipped in the same manner as the quota of
such state, unless the legislature of such state shall judge
that such extra number cannot be safely spared out of
the same, in which case they shall raise, officer, cloath,
arm and equip as many of such extra number as they

judge can be safely spared. And the officers and men
so cloathed, armed and equipped, shall march to the
place appointed, and within the time agreed on by the
united states in congress assembled.

The united states in congress assembled shall never
engage in a war, nor grant letters of marque and reprisal
in time of peace, nor enter into any treaties or alliances,
nor coin money, nor regulate the value thereof, nor ascertain the sums and expences necessary for the defence
and welfare of the united states, or any of them, nor
emit bills, nor borrow money on the credit of the united
states, nor appropriate money, nor agree upon the number of vessels of war, to be built or purchased, or the
number of land or sea forces to be raised, nor appoint
a commander in chief of the army or navy, unless nine
states assent to the same: nor shall a question on any
other point, except for adjourning from day to day be determined, unless by the votes of a majority of the united
states in congress assembled.

The congress of the united states shall have power to
adjourn to any time within the year, and to any place
within the united states, so that no period of adjourn-
ment be for a longer duration than the space of six
Months, and shall publish the Journal of their proceedings monthly, except such parts thereof relating to treaties, alliances or military operations as in their judgment
require secresy; and the yeas and nays of the delegates
of each state on any question shall be entered on the
Journal, when it is desired by any delegate; and the
delegates of a state, or any of them, at his or their
request shall be furnished with a transcript of the said

Journal, except such parts as are above excepted, to lay before the legislatures of the several states.

Art. X. The committee of the states, or any nine of them, shall be authorised to execute, in the recess of congress, such of the powers of congress as the united states in congress assembled, by the consent of nine states, shall from time to time think expedient .to vest them with; provided that no power be delegated to the said committee, for the exercise of which by the articles of confederation, the voice of nine states in the congress of the united states assembled is requisite.

Art. XI. Canada acceding to this confederation, and joining in the measures of the united states, shall be admitted into, and entitled to all the advantages of this union: but no other colony shall be admitted into the same, unless such admission be agreed to by nine states.

Art. XII. All bills of credit emitted, monies borrowed and debts contracted by, or under the authority of congress, before the assembling of the united states, in pursuance of the present confederation, shall be deemed and considered as a charge against the united states, for payment and satisfaction whereof the said united states, and the public faith are hereby solemnly pledged.

Art. XIII. Every state shall abide by the determinations of the united states in congress assembled, on all questions which by this confederation are submitted to them. And the Articles of this confederation shall be inviolably observed by every state, and the union shall be perpetual; nor shall any alteration at any time hereafter be made in any of them; unless such alteration be agreed to in a congress of the united states, and be afterwards confirmed by the legislatures of every state.

AND WHEREAS it hath pleased the Great Governor of the World to incline the hearts of the legislatures we respectively represent in congress, to approve of, and to authorize us to ratify the said articles of confederation and perpetual union. KNOW YE that we the undersigned delegates, by virtue of the power and authority to us given for that purpose, do by these presents, in the name and in behalf of our respective constituents, fully and entirely ratify and confirm each and every of the said articles of confederation and perpetual union, and all and singular the matters and things therein contained: And we do further solemnly plight and engage the faith of our respective constituents, that they shall abide by the determinations of the united states in congress assembled, on all questions, which by the said confederation are submitted to them. And that the articles thereof shall be inviolably observed by the states we respectively represent, and that the union shall be perpetual. In Witness thereof we have hereunto set our hands in Congress. Done at Philadelphia in the state of Pennsylvania the ninth Day of July in the Year of our Lord one Thousand seven Hundred and Seventy-eight, and in the third year of the independence of America.

JOSIAH BARTLETT
JOHN WENTWORTH Junr } On the part & behalf of the
   August 8th 1778   State of New Hampshire

JOHN HANCOCK
SAMUEL ADAMS
ELBRIDGE GERRY   } On the part and behalf of
FRANCIS DANA   The State of Massachusetts
JAMES LOVELL   Bay
SAMUEL HOLTEN

WILLIAM ELLERY
HENRY MARCHANT   } On the part and behalf of the
JOHN COLLINS   State of Rhode-Island and
                         Providence Plantations

ROGER SHERMAN
SAMUEL HUNTINGTON
OLIVER WOLCOTT   } On the part and behalf of the
TITUS HOSMER   State of Connecticut
ANDREW ADAMS

JA^S DUANE
FRA^S LEWIS   } On the Part and Behalf of the
W^M DUER   State of New York
GOUV MORRIS

JNO WITHERSPOON   } On the Part and in Behalf of
NATH^L SCUDDER   the State of New Jersey.
                         Novr 26, 1778.—

ROB^T MORRIS
DANIEL ROBERDEAU
JON^A BAYARD SMITH   } On the part and behalf of the
WILLIAM CLINGAN   State of Pennsylvania
JOSEPH REED   22^d July
   1778

THO M:KEAN   Feby 12
   1779
JOHN DICKINSON   May 5th } On the part &°behalf of the
   1779   State of Delaware
NICHOLAS VAN DYKE

JOHN HANSON   March 1   } On the part and behalf of the
   1781   State of Maryland
DANIEL CARROLL d°

RICHARD HENRY LEE
JOHN BANISTER
THOMAS ADAMS   } On the Part and Behalf of the
JN^O HARVIE   State of Virginia
FRANCIS LIGHTFOOT LEE

JOHN PENN   July 21st 1778
CORNS HARNETT
JNO WILLIAMS
} On the part and Behalf of the State of No Carolina

HENRY LAURENS
WILLIAM HENRY DRAYTON
JNO MATHEWS
RICHD HUTSON
THOS HEYWARD   Junr
} On the part & behalf of the State of South-Carolina

JNO WALTON   24th July 1778
EDWD TELFAIR
EDWD LANGWORTHY
} On the part & behalf of the State of Georgia

INDEX